THE MODERN ORACLE

BECOMING MORE PSYCHIC

INTIMATE SECRETS TO ENHANCE YOUR INTUITIVE GIFTS

Katy-K

International Award-Winning Psychic

First published by Ultimate World Publishing 2023
Copyright © 2023 Katy-K

ISBN

Paperback: 978-1-922828-85-9
Ebook: 978-1-922828-86-6

Katy-K has asserted her rights under the Copyright, Designs and Patents Act 1988 to be identified as the author of this work. The information in this book is based on the author's experiences and opinions. The publisher specifically disclaims responsibility for any adverse consequences which may result from use of the information contained herein. Permission to use information has been sought by the author. Any breaches will be rectified in further editions of the book.

All rights reserved. No part of this publication may be reproduced, stored in or introduced into a retrieval system, or transmitted in any form, or by any means (electronic, mechanical, photocopying, recording or otherwise) without the prior written permission of the author. Any person who does any unauthorised act in relation to this publication may be liable to criminal prosecution and civil claims for damages. Enquiries should be made through the publisher.

Cover design: Ultimate World Publishing
Layout and typesetting: Ultimate World Publishing
Editor: Anita Saunders

Ultimate World Publishing
Diamond Creek,
Victoria Australia 3089
www.writeabook.com.au

Testimonials

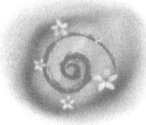

A window into the everyday adventures of a modern-day psychic that reminds us there is a bit of psychic in us all. Katy-K breaks down the illusions associated with the psychic and spiritual world and brings modern-day readers face to face with what everyday happenings look, feel and sound like in the life of a psychic. Surprising moments with clients and everyday encounters reveal the potential for spiritual awareness and development. Katy-K reveals the curiosity, empathy and heartfelt desire to connect that lead her on the path to being more psychic through recount and a dash of humour. She shares her crazy, psychic life in such a way that makes you want to read more and more. A fabulous read that definitely 'enlightens one on what can happen on the path to becoming more psychic'.

Jules Impiccini
Educator, Writer, Spiritualist

I was engaged in Katy's book from the first paragraph as I had often wondered what life as a psychic was like. I loved the warmth and humour of the book, which made it enjoyable to read. Katy's honesty and humility about her psychic gift and the experiences she has had along the way were inspiring for a novice psychic.

Georgie Rowe
Creativity and Resilience Coach

I was thrilled when Katy-K announced her second book! Her first book, *The Modern Oracle: How to Tap Into Your Unique Psychic Powers*, left me wanting more. I found great lessons and enjoyed the messages in her retelling of events and how she has been guided and shown what to use her abilities for. What a fascinating journey Katy-K's life of learning and development of her psychic abilities is for herself and her family, with some events that are laugh-out-loud funny and show the unexpected events that affect the household.
Naturally, it left me wanting to know more.
Well done, Katy-K.
Another excellent read.

Meredith
South Australia

I'm so glad I had the opportunity to read this! Just like in her first book, Katy-K draws the reader in with her authenticity and beautiful personality, and shares the most amazing and hilarious stories from her life as a psychic. An excellent read!

Anita Saunders
Editor

Dedication

I dedicate this book to my family and friends and all the people who have assisted me on my journey. You all know who you are!

With love and deep gratitude for your love, encouragement and support.

Blessings to you all

Katy-K

Contents

Testimonials	iii
Dedication	v
Preface	1
Introduction	3
Believe	7
The Empath	17
The Healer	31
Energy	41
The Right Path	59
'Hogwarts'	71
Messages and Visitations	87
Hauntings	93
Readings	101
Challenges	115
Becoming More Psychic	139
Testimonials	143
Offers	157
Contact Details for Katy-K	159
About the Author	161
Speakers Bio	163

Preface

Many people wonder about the lives of psychics: about what happens and what can happen. Have you ever wondered about the life of a psychic? Have you ever found yourself pondering about how psychics connect and the strange and crazy world of psychic abilities and happenings?

While writing my first book, *The Modern Oracle – How To Tap Into Your Unique Psychic Powers*, it soon became obvious that there was way too much material for one book, so many unexplainable and crazy happenings that most would find incredible, unbelievable, and so the idea for this book was born.

My first book included insights into the many levels of spiritual development that led to becoming an award-winning international psychic medium. It demonstrated how I proved the purpose of the many steps necessary to propel the developing intuitive forward on their spiritual path: a path that can lead to doing psychic readings and more.

The Modern Oracle II

I remember my publisher laughing as I recounted some of the crazy stories and commenting that people will want to know about all these crazy experiences, but they should go in your next book.

Initially, the title of this book was going to be *The Modern Oracle – My Crazy Psychic Life* because it has been a crazy journey that I can mostly look back on with awe and sometimes humour.

I am a psychic medium, and not only do I offer guidance, but I also teach people how to develop their intuitive gifts, how to become more psychic.

My journey certainly didn't end with my first book, and there are many more experiences to share that can continue to assist others on their spiritual path, hence the sequel. Through recounting some of my experiences, I am endeavouring to teach what most psychics wish they had known sooner as they progressed on their journey: the secrets to becoming more psychic.

My passion for becoming more psychic drives me to continue to learn from some of the best in the business and travel far and wide across the globe to achieve this. I then teach the most useful, proven insights to assist with a speedy progression.

To this day, I still want constant and never-ending improvement that can lead to becoming a more powerful psychic healer and to share the journey with others. Why? Because that is what psychics do: we share and guide. We support the grief-stricken, the overwhelmed and anyone needing guidance to continue on their chosen path.

I hope you will enjoy this book and continue to learn from the experiences and teachings and when you are ready to explore further, you might like to check out my website www.katy-k.com where there are many opportunities to assist you with becoming more psychic.

Introduction

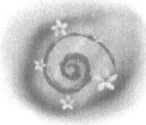

When people ask me about my psychic journey, I say it has been crazy, uncontrollable, addictive and mostly fun. I mean, I never dreamed that a naked man would turn up to one of my classes and that one of the most common questions I would be asked would be,

"Is my dead grandmother watching me have sex?"

If you had told me 20 years ago that I would watch a table walk across a room, I would not have believed it was possible and probably would have had thoughts along the lines of, *hmm ... I wonder if they are making this up,* or *maybe they have gone off their medication.* I mean, these are not everyday occurrences, but they can be in the life of a psychic.

Tony, my poor 'muggle' husband, didn't know that I was a psychic when he married me, and sometimes I wonder if he knew back then how crazy life could get, would he have run for the hills? Nor would he have thought that he would ever ask me the following question:

The Modern Oracle II

"Have you brought your work home with you again?"

He was suggesting that the client's family in spirit may have followed me home, all because the television turned off unaided, the lights started flickering or strange unexplained noises were occurring. Living with a psychic is sometimes not for the faint-hearted, but he must love me as he is still here and has become quite blasé about the 'weird shit' that happens, as he puts it.

One night while looking for a hotel to book for our trip away, he enquired if I would like to stay in a particular hotel because it was the best price available. I replied sarcastically, "Do you want to get any sleep?" He was enquiring about a hotel where we have been haunted every visit.

If you are curious about the life of a psychic and what can happen when you develop your intuitive gifts, then you are reading the right book.

Within the content, you will find that I have covered a broad range of topics, and I will share experiences that have helped me to uncover new intuitive gifts and what is possible when you are psychic. Secrets will be revealed as to how I upgrade my energy, the different ways I heal others and how 'psychic amnesia' can affect some clients. The secret that won't be revealed is the true identity of some people in this book as I endeavour to protect their privacy.

You will discover that many psychics don't believe in themselves and may continually feel like an impostor. Impostor Syndrome can hinder the development of psychics. I have included a quiz for you to do so you can check if you have this syndrome.

A spiritual path can be challenging to navigate when there is no clear map to guide you to your final destination, wherever it happens to

Introduction

be. Most of us set off blindly, oblivious to the many bumps, detours, challenges and craziness we will encounter along the way.

For some of us, it can feel like we are on a hamster wheel continually travelling in circles, unaware that we are not progressing forward and oblivious to anything outside the wheel.

There are always things we may encounter along the way that drive us nuts, the negative and the unexpected. Then upon reflection, we realise that those challenging lessons prepare us for more extensive lessons yet to come.

Did I know what I was doing on my journey? No! I have just continually stumbled along the path, looking for the signs and synchronicities to indicate that I was on the right path as I sought ways to enhance my intuitive gifts further. Miraculously, I sometimes ended up in the right places at the right time and meeting the right people, which led to unique opportunities for expansion.

If you'd asked me 20 years ago if I would have produced two oracle decks, a book and be working on a second book, I would've thought you were crazy. I now know that this all was part of my journey.

Being an empath contributes to the craziness in my life, and it sure makes life interesting when you have the ability sometimes to mirror the pain and emotions of others. Recently I suffered morning sickness at the same time as our pregnant daughter, who lives more than three hours away. I was complaining about how I had felt nauseous the last few days, and she said she had too. It soon stopped after receiving her confirmation that she was the cause of it, and she said, "Gosh, Mum, I hope you don't have to go through the labour too."

The Modern Oracle II

This book is about my experiences on my way to becoming more psychic, some of them crazy, and many pertinent to my evolution into the psychic I am today. Looking back, I can see that quite a few experiences would unveil new intuitive abilities that had been lying dormant until needed or tested. These experiences were the first inkling of what was to come: intuitive gifts to explore, ones that I had initially ignored and that continued to occur until I took notice.

Becoming more psychic is a subject I take seriously, but it would be remiss of me if I didn't share all the humorous stories too. I do hope you enjoy a glimpse into the life of a working psychic.

Believe

In the early stages of your development, you may not always comprehend what you are experiencing or its relevance. With experience comes knowledge.

Over the years, I have had many 'psychic' experiences, some of which have been more memorable than others. Experiences that I considered contributed to the realisation of a new or existing skill. I would realise later that these incidents were all part of my journey, and each experience was like a building block or a stepping stone that made me stronger, enhanced my intuitive gifts and built my confidence.

If You Are Psychic, Why Can't You Tell Me the Winning Lotto Numbers?

I often get asked, can you tell me the winning lotto numbers? When they ask, it is mainly jovial, but my answer always remains the same … No!

The Modern Oracle II

Imagine if I could tell people the lotto numbers, and the word got around. I would be in such demand that I wouldn't have a life, and I am sure those in charge of the lottery would get suspicious if suddenly all my family and friends were winning large amounts of money. Many would want the winning numbers, and some might not be nice about it.

My friend Alex has an intuitive gift, but he doesn't really buy into the 'woo-woo' stuff. I find he is a classic example of someone with one or both of the following: 'If you don't believe in it, then it isn't so' or 'I will believe it when I see it' syndromes. Yeah, they are not 'real' syndromes that I know of, just ones I often witness.

In Alex's case, I think he has both sometimes. He has intuitives in his family, so you would think he would be totally on board with the whole psychic thing, but he is not. We have both lived in different environments, and he lived in a country with a different culture, and I believe psychics are not part of that culture. Over the years I witnessed his opinion and beliefs change as he became more sceptical.

One day, while having lunch with Alex at a beachside hotel, he suggested we check out the horse races on the nearby television. I have no interest in horse racing, but as we talked, I could see he was distracted by the television and the betting section where you could place a bet on horses in the different races.

As he looked at the television, Alex asked, "Have a look at the horses, and tell me which one you think is going to win?"

"I don't want to, as it won't work," I quietly replied. I believed that choosing winning horses was not in my skill set.

"Have a bit of confidence?" he said. "Show me what you can do."

I looked at the television screen and chose a horse. "Don't back it," I said, "or it won't win."

I watched him closely as he decided to do as I suggested. Then that horse won the race.

"Have another go, Kate. Tell me which horse you think will win this time," he requested as he pushed me a bit more teasingly.

I was starting to get a little anxious, as my ego was hooking in, and I was worried about disappointing Alex by being wrong. With more encouragement, I selected another horse and then anxiously watched the horse win its race.

This went on for a couple more races, with Alex asking me to select a horse I thought might win and then waiting for a result. I also reminded him several times that I felt that if we backed the horses that I selected, we would not win.

After selecting another horse for the next race, I went off to visit the bathroom and when I returned, I discovered that my chosen horse had lost its race. *Oh well, the winning streak could not last forever*, I thought. Followed by, *I wonder if Alex backed that horse?*

"Alex, did you back that horse?" I asked suspiciously.

"I couldn't resist," he replied. "I can't understand why it didn't win like all the other horses you selected did."

"The horse didn't win because you backed it. I told you not to back it. Don't ask me why, but I knew that if you backed a horse I suggested, the horse would lose."

"Why on earth would that happen?" he enquired.

"I don't exactly know. It is just how it seems to work with me," I answered.

"But why, Kate? Surely you don't believe that because I bet on the horse it lost?" he asked.

"I don't know, Alex, but I know I had a feeling that you shouldn't back a horse I suggested if you wanted it to win. I think that this whole testing session that you have just put me through was to prove to you that it is possible," I replied. The game was over, and I refused to choose any more horses. I quickly changed the subject and asked him a question about his work.

Later I decided to connect to my guides to seek answers, so I could understand why the situation happened the way it did that afternoon and to find out why the horse would lose if we bet on it.

The following explanation came through. *If the horse had won the race that Alex had bet on, you would put yourself in a position where others would come to rely on you to select winners. This is not what your gift is for. You would have no time for the work you are meant to do. Eventually, you would have much pressure put upon you to succeed in this area and perhaps that would lead you on a different spiritual path. We showed you what you could do to gain confidence, as Alex suggested, but not for either of you to make a living from it. Your gift is not meant for gambling. Using your intuitive gift for healing and not personal gain is more beneficial.*

Even though Alex is sceptical about 'psychics', he sometimes asks me to check out certain things. Years ago, upon his request, I checked out some photos of a few of his employees and possibly future employees.

He wanted advice on which ones I thought were genuine and a good fit for his business. Even though he said he would take my advice on board, I felt that he didn't perceive the information to be psychic advice.

I Don't Believe in What You Do, but Can You Find My Wallet?

One of the groomsmen lost his wallet the day after my brother's wedding. With the help of some of his friends, they had searched the room he had stayed in and anywhere else he had been. My mother decided I should be able to find the missing wallet and announced, "Kathryn is psychic; get her to tell you where the wallet is."

I was horrified. We were with a bunch of sceptics and people who did not understand how psychics worked. *Oh no, I can't believe she said that*, I thought, as they all looked at me sceptically. Then I thought, *I don't have to prove anything, and this could go pear-shaped if I don't find the wallet, and then I will look silly.*

My insecurities were kicking in, but my mother truly believed I could do it. I am generally not the lost-and-found psychic; I don't consider it one of my skills.

Everyone was now looking for the wallet, and someone said, "Go on, Kate, see if you can find the wallet," in a challenging way, and again all eyes were on me.

Without thinking, I pointed my finger at the couch and stated, "It is under the cushion of that couch."

My dad was sitting on the couch and quickly lifted the cushion, and there was the wallet. I was surprised. The guy was happy to have his wallet back, and everyone returned to what they were doing before the search. Even after that proof, some didn't want to accept what had just occurred and viewed it as a lucky guess.

From experience, I know that those who are not ready to believe that others are intuitive will find ways to justify or disprove the unexplainable and incomprehensible.

Excuse Me, Is That Naked Man Your Husband?

My business started to expand with the availability of Skype. These days I prefer to use Zoom, and I am sure that as technology keeps advancing, there will be more platforms that work even better to communicate with others. Skype became an excellent tool that allowed me to teach anyone, anywhere in the world, as long as they had internet access.

Years ago, I was teaching one of my many students on Skype who was not quite perceiving how Skype worked and was learning a new way of communicating. For the first few sessions, I coached her to line her face up with the laptop camera instead of the ceiling light; she was that new to Skype.

She loved her lessons and commented that she looked forward to her weekly session with me.

One day during a session, she was required to connect to someone known to me in spirit for the first time. All her classes to date had been leading up to this point, and she was nervous but excited. Clare (not her real name) was sitting in silence with her eyes closed while I waited for her to bring someone through. Then I saw movement directly behind her as a tall, well-built naked man walked into the large room towards what looked like a laundry basket. In my head, I thought, *surely this is not happening!* I then witnessed him bend over while he had his back to me to get something out of the basket.

Clare, who still had her eyes closed, was oblivious to what was happening behind her. I quickly decided that I should bring her attention to the naked man behind her, before I saw any more than I had already seen. You all know what you see when a naked man bends over that far, or if anyone naked bends over that far.

"Clare, there's a naked man behind you," I said quickly.

"Who do you think it is, and do you know him?" she replied, hopeful that she had made a connection.

"Well, I don't know him, but I am hoping you do," I answered.

"So, you don't know who he is? I really am trying to bring through someone known to you. Are you sure you don't know who it is?" Clare further questioned hopefully while starting to sound frustrated.

"I am certain that I don't know who he is. I am sure I would remember him if I did," I answered and smiled.

At this stage, I twigged that she thought I was seeing someone in spirit, and I suppose that it was feasible for her to believe that, considering the exercise we were doing. She later confessed that she thought I was seeing what she failed to see while trying to connect to the spirit world.

"Clare, I think you should look behind you, as this looks like a real naked man, and I definitely don't know who he is, but I am hoping that you do," I instructed with urgency.

With that, she turned around and shrieked, "Jeffrey, put some clothes on; Katy can see you."

Jeffrey then, at that point, turned around and questioned, "Where's Katy? There is no one here." I now saw a full-frontal version of Jeffrey and was trying not to look or laugh. I mean, no man likes anyone to laugh when they see him naked; it is not good for their ego!

"She is on Skype. Quickly put some clothes on," she beseeched.

With great urgency, Jeffrey covered himself with the piece of clothing he had just pulled out of the basket and hightailed it out of the room.

"OMG, Katy," she said as she put her head in her hands. "I am so sorry that you had to see that. I never expected that to happen. I think my husband must have thought that I was talking on the phone. Otherwise, he would never have come into the room naked."

From that point, it was difficult to focus and get back into the lesson as we both laughed about what had just occurred, and I assured Clare that I wasn't offended.

"You know that this story will end up in a book one day," I stated to Clare.

"It was funny," she replied while shaking her head. "As long as you don't use our real names, I don't mind."

"No, I won't be using real names," I assured. "I don't know if anyone would believe what just happened."

"I know; I just can't believe it happened," she said while laughing. "I thought I had successfully brought through someone you knew and was wondering how I did it and why they would turn up naked. This is so funny. Has it happened to you before?"

"Never before; this is the first time. I would love to tell you that this is the 'norm' in my lessons. What entertainment do you have for me during your next lesson?" I jokingly asked.

"I don't think anything can top that," she replied with a grin.

Clare continued to learn from me for quite a while and developed into an excellent medium. I am sure neither of us will ever forget that session. It was certainly not something I could have ever envisaged happening. Clare also mentioned that upon discussing the incident with Jeffrey, he confirmed that he thought she was talking on the phone and found it hilarious that he had managed to shock her teacher.

The Empath

Sometimes It Sucks to Be a Clairsentient

Are you clairsentient?

Have you ever heard the phrase "I feel your pain?" Do you think it is possible to feel what others feel?

Until I started literally feeling other people's pain, I thought it was just something people say to confirm that they could relate to what you were explaining. As I have a 'blanket' request with my spirit team to prove everything, I go through life having experiences that turn me from a sceptic to a believer.

My daughter Chloe and I have an exceptionally close bond. So close that I get to feel what she feels when she is unwell, and it is even stronger when we are together. If I sit beside her and she has sinus pain, then I have sinus pain. Now, this doesn't happen all the time, and I am unsure why it is so random, but I assume it happens because I am being made aware that an issue should be dealt with.

One day while sitting next to Chloe in the passenger seat of her car, my head started to ache, and the pain quickly worsened. The pain was so intense that my face paled, and I was concerned that I would throw up.

"What's wrong, Mum?" Chloe asked as she looked over at me.

"I have this dreadful headache that has come on since I got in your car. Maybe it is something in your car causing it," I replied as I looked around the car for the culprit.

"Mum, is the pain in this part of your head?" Chloe enquired as she touched the top of her forehead.

"Yes, Chloe, that is exactly where it is," I replied.

"My pain is in the same area, and I am nauseous too. It is my sinuses."

Chloe had been diagnosed with chronic sinusitis and polyps due to a trauma in that area a few years prior.

"If it's not your pain, can't you just ask the spirit world to take it away?" she enquired.

I had taught Chloe to communicate the following to her spirit team whenever she is in pain … "If this is not my pain, then take it away."

"Believe me, I have, Chloe, and it's just not going away, which leads me to believe that as I am feeling your pain, then you need to do something about it quickly," I answered.

"I am seeing the specialist on Monday, and hopefully, something can be done about it," she replied.

"I am so sorry that you feel like this a lot of the time, Chloe; that is not right. I am feeling for you," I sympathised.

A week later, Chloe was booked in for sinus surgery.

I Feel Your Pain

On another occasion, I woke up one morning with persistent stomach pain. Tony suggested that maybe it was a bowel issue, but I wasn't convinced. The pain continued to grow throughout the day, but never got to the unbearable stage. I was confident that I didn't have anything seriously wrong with me and, to Tony's disgust, wouldn't go to see a doctor, preferring to wait to see if the pain worsened before bothering anyone.

That afternoon Chloe called to say that in the morning, she had awoken to severe pain in her abdomen that worsened as the day progressed. She was now at times doubling over in pain.

"Mum, do you think my stomach pain is something serious? Should I book in to see a doctor?"

"Chloe, I have had discomfort in my stomach all day, and I don't think anything is wrong with me. My pain is certainly nothing like what you are experiencing. I think I am mirroring your pain, and because of that, I think you need to go to the hospital and get checked out," I stressed.

"Mum, I don't want to go to the hospital; I am so over it. I hate going to the hospital," Chloe complained. I could understand how she felt as she had become a frequent hospital patient in the last few years.

"Chloe, this could be very serious; you should call for an ambulance straight away," I urged.

"I think I will wait until Sam gets home, and he can take me to the hospital," Chloe replied.

"Chloe, seriously, I think you better go to the hospital immediately," I repeated.

Of course, Chloe didn't call an ambulance, so by the time she did get to the hospital, she was in excruciating pain and had to have emergency surgery for several issues, including having her appendix removed. As soon as Chloe received medical attention, my pain went away.

Another time, I was visiting Chloe, and we were both sitting on the couch watching a movie with Tony. Chloe went to the bathroom, and when she returned and sat next to me, I started feeling jittery and restless. It felt like I had ants crawling through me, and I just wanted to get up and move. Unbeknownst to me, Chloe had just taken a double dose of Ventolin (for asthma), and I was feeling the effects of it. When she explained that they were the effects she was feeling, I moved to the other side of Tony on the couch and was no longer affected. It appears that Tony was a good shield, and I suspect that is because he is so grounded. I also mentioned to Chloe that she must have taken too much Ventolin for me to feel that way.

The above experiences are only a few of the many that I have shared with Chloe. Typically, it can be what an empath can experience at times. I believe that I experience Chloe's health issues as a warning, mainly when they are serious, and it confirms that there is a problem. Sometimes it just highlights our strong bond.

The Empath

All of these experiences have proven to me that an empath/clairsentient can experience symptoms of those they have a connection with. At first, you may not comprehend why you have the experience. Many of you will learn to distinguish whether the symptoms relate to you or someone you are close to.

I Feel Your Energy

Both our adult children live in Brisbane, which is close to a four-hour car journey for them to drive to where we live. Sometimes it can take six hours if there is a hold-up in the traffic. Yet, without even knowing the exact time they set out on their journey to visit us or how many pit stops they had on the way, it is not uncommon for me to 'feel' when they arrive. It can be a knowing in my head that 'they are here' or feeling a change in energy. Then I will be drawn to the front door just as they turn into our driveway or have just parked the car.

Years ago, on one of my trips to England to attend Arthur Findlay College (known as AFC), my Aunty Joy and Uncle George, who are like another set of parents, decided to travel with me. They felt safer making the long journey with me accompanying them, and they were looking forward to going on an extended bus tour around the UK. After a few days in London showing them around, they set off on their bus tour, and I went to college. I didn't know their exact itinerary, just that they were going to different parts of the United Kingdom, and I trusted they would be safe.

The plan was that Tony would fly to England after I finished college to meet with me and drive around the UK for a week on a bit of a sightseeing holiday in a rented car. Then we were going to meet up with George and Joy in London at the end of their bus tour and escort them to Rome.

It was the last day of our trip, and Tony and I were driving from Glastonbury to London. As we were driving along, I saw a Stonehenge sign and said to Tony, "I think George and Joy are at Stonehenge."

"Why do you say that?" he asked.

"I just feel like they are," I replied.

"I doubt it. It is doubtful they would be there right at this very time," he scoffed.

"Seriously, I can feel them; they are close by. Let's stop in at Stonehenge and surprise them," I begged. Then I thought, *gosh, I hope they are there, or I will never live it down if I am wrong.*

We pulled into the car park at Stonehenge, and I excitedly jumped out of the car. I then found them within a few minutes, to everyone's surprise, including my own.

"I'm so surprised to see you two; how did you know we were here?" Joy asked in astonishment.

I jokingly replied, "You can't get away from me; I'll find you!"

I believe it is possible to feel the energy of others, especially when you have a connection, but in my experience, stress can block this ability.

It Is Not Unusual for Empaths to Feel Depressed

It is not unusual for psychics, especially empaths, to feel depressed. Sometimes there can be this feeling of the whole world swallowing you up or a feeling of being overwhelmed. Just imagine each day you are working with a client; you get to feel what they are feeling for the time you are with them. Some may say that you should protect yourself better. It is not about how well you energetically protect yourself. Part of the 'deal' when you are an empath is being able to connect to the client; therefore, you may get to feel what they feel. If you were claircognizant, you would just know. But clairsentients and empaths get to feel everything.

Be Careful Who You Get Into Bed With

One of my students was concerned that she was suffering from depression, but she only felt depressed when she first awoke in the morning. Then once she had left the bedroom, she would feel okay for the rest of the day. After tuning in to her energy, I asked if her partner was depressed, and she confirmed he had chronic depression. Their connection was such that, as an empath, she would mirror his state of mind. I suggested that she energetically protect herself and clear her energy when necessary.

Now imagine how it is if you are an empath connecting to someone who has bipolar disorder; your moods could frequently change. That is why empaths/clairsentients can sometimes be seen as moody. Their mood can change like the wind and be determined by the people near them and what their mood is. Empaths sometimes project the feelings of others and not only the living but the deceased as well.

Clearing and protecting your energy is essential for clairsentients and the information on how to do this is available in my first book.

It is not unusual for clairsentients to react before something happens as they may be intuitively picking up on what is yet to come.

You Are Giving Me a Migraine

My sister Jules came to stay for a night to break up her journey on her way to Brisbane, and I was excited that we would get to spend some time together catching up. We have a close connection, and it is not unusual for me to pick up on any ailments she may have.

Jules looked tired and stressed, and as we chatted, I got a headache that progressed into a severe migraine. I didn't want to abandon Jules as we only had that night to catch up, but nothing was working to take the pain away, and as it got too much for me, I had to go to bed. The headache lingered until she left the next day. Her energy appeared to be affecting me, which was a sign that she was not in good health. When we spoke about it later, she felt terrible for causing me to feel unwell, and it concerned her that it had happened. I reassured her that this experience further highlighted our special connection.

Clairsentients Are Sensitive to More Than Feelings

I have found that many clairsentients have food allergies and intolerances. They can also be susceptible to chemicals and pesticides. I know that is certainly the case for me. When I am around pesticides, my mouth will go tingly or numb, and even my lips will swell. I will react even if the pesticides are used by others nearby.

Clairsentients can be sensitive to certain foods. Whilst fish and seafood are supposed to be healthy and good for you, it is not so for me as my body reacts like I have been poisoned and rejects it not long after it is ingested. My daughter also has the same problem.

As I age, I am finding that I am becoming even more sensitive to many things. Certain smells will be overpowering and cause headaches or nausea. Loud noises hurt my ears. I am the person who wears special earplugs to Zumba as the music is too loud for me. At first, I thought they were playing the music too loud, but after asking others, I was the only one affected by the sound level.

Years ago, after a dental procedure, I awoke the following day to a tight feeling around my mouth, only to discover that my lips were so swollen that my top lip was touching my nose. Our son John, who was only seven years old at the time, innocently commented that I looked like a 'muppet', and with that, I burst into tears. This was all before it was popular to inject stuff into your lips to make them bigger. Imagine that! I was accidentally ahead of time. My dentist was shocked as she had never encountered anything like this before and immediately wrote out a script for medication to help reduce the swelling. It took days for the swelling to go down, and when I went out in public, people would blatantly stare as my lips looked that bad. We didn't find what caused the swelling, but it was evident to the dentist that I had a rare allergic reaction. My body was becoming more and more sensitive.

The above experiences are a glimpse of what is possible when you are a clairsentient or an empath.

SOS

Something didn't feel right. I was sitting at my desk updating my diary when suddenly, I felt a little unsettled and then in my head was an image of Howard's face flashing on and off. Howard is my dear friend Marilla's husband. *Why do I see Howard's face?* I wondered. *There must be something wrong!* A minute later, I picked up my phone and called Marilla. As soon as she answered her phone, I hurriedly asked, "How is Howard?"

"He has just been stung by a jellyfish and is in a lot of pain. We are swimming on the beach at Noosa Heads, and he got stung across his chest," Marilla replied.

"Oh no! I will let you go; please keep me informed," I added.

"Will do," she answered.

I ended the call and prayed for Howard to be safe and heal quickly. I have been best friends with Marilla for more than 34 years, and she is like a wonderful sister to me. We chuckle whenever we reminisce about the above incident and recall the shock of her receiving my call just minutes after he was stung, and Howard's total surprise and incredulity. What had happened to Howard was not life-threatening, but it was painful, and I had been spiritually notified for some reason. The only conclusion I can come to as to why I was notified is that maybe it was to provide further evidence for Howard (who is a sceptic and 'muggle') that, *hey, there might be something in this 'woo-woo' thing and maybe Katy is not crazy after all!*

Over the years, some questionable instances have happened around Howard that have confused him. He is not someone who is just going to accept things at face value, and he is not the only one. As psychics have never been a part of his life, his analytical brain questions everything. I am lucky he tolerates my seemingly 'weird' mannerisms.

The Magic Phone

Another incident involving Howard was when he, Marilla, Tony and I went on a lovely cruise around the Caribbean. One evening, while we were out at sea, an image of Chloe's face popped into my mind, followed by my phone ringing. I was a little surprised as in those days there was no phone service for passengers once we were out at sea, and the ship's Wi-Fi was very expensive, slow and you had to pay by the minute.

I answered the phone, and to my surprise, it was Chloe. She needed her mum for some nurturing and support. As we talked, I made my way to where the others were waiting for me, and they were surprised to see me talking on the phone.

"What are you doing?" Tony asked.

"Just talking to Chloe; she needed to talk to me," I replied.

"How are you getting service?" he questioned as they checked out their phones to see if they could get service.

"I don't know; my phone rang, and I answered it," I replied.

"Chloe, would you like to talk to your dad?" I asked.

"Yes, please, Mum," Chloe replied.

I handed the phone over to Tony, and he spoke with Chloe for a while before handing the phone back to me.

"How are you getting service?" Marilla asked.

"I don't know; my phone just is," I answered.

"None of our phones are getting service; strangely, yours is. Can I see your phone for a minute to check it out?" Howard asked.

The Modern Oracle II

I handed over my phone to Howard and watched him check my phone settings and compare them to his phone settings. He could not find why my phone was receiving service, and no one else's was. He questioned me further while he tried to solve the mystery as the situation was unexplainable, and his analytical mind could not get his head around it.

"Is there anyone you would like to call? Would you like to phone your daughters?" I offered to Marilla and Howard.

"Maybe it won't work for me," Marilla replied, as she knows how different things can be in my world.

"Here, give it a go; you have nothing to lose," I offered as I handed over my phone to her. Marilla then called and had a lengthy conversation with one of their daughters. Meanwhile, Howard was still looking confused and trying to work out how he could get his phone to make calls; Tony was not fazed at all.

"I wouldn't bother trying to work it out. This sort of stuff happens all the time," Tony laughingly said.

"Just enjoy the phone," I added.

When the last call was made with my phone, it was returned to me, and Marilla said,

"You had better keep this phone; it is amazing."

Of course, I didn't keep the phone. If I had kept that phone, it currently would not be able to accept any software updates. It was not the phone that was behind Chloe getting through to me. It was the power of the bond we have and the spirit world enabling the connection.

The Empath

I have discovered that it is not always possible to comprehend how and why something occurs. If it is meant to happen, the spirit world will enable it. There will always be sceptics, and accepting the unexplainable is not always possible for some.

The Healer

Sharing the Gift of Healing

'Healing Mandalas'

I was a teenager when I channelled my first 'healing' mandala. At the time, I didn't know exactly what I was doing. I mainly channelled them in my most boring class at high school, 'Citizen Education' (think politics). At 15 years of age, I had zero interest in politics, so I would often 'zone' out (which was a form of an altered state for me) and draw mandalas. It was no surprise that I always failed this subject.

Sometimes, I would find myself thinking of a person while drawing a mandala, only to discover later that the person who had popped into my mind had been unwell at that time and then went on to heal quickly. Looking back, I genuinely believe that the power of the channelled mandalas I was drawing enabled a speedy recovery.

At the time, I thought I was doodling on paper because I was bored. Every mandala I drew was different and not symmetrical; mandalas are usually symmetrical. The imperfections mirrored the need for healing, and the shapes and symbols within the mandala were all part of the healing. I also noticed that if I was unwell, feeling down or out of sorts in some way that drawing a mandala soon picked me up and made me feel better. At that time, I didn't realise the true significance of the mandalas I was drawing.

Once I left school and entered the 'fast lane' of life, I ceased to channel the healing mandalas. It wasn't until what I call my 'rebirth' and reconnection to my intuitive gifts that I was compelled to draw healing mandalas again. The desire usually came after I had been meditating or connected to the spirit world in some way.

The first mandalas I drew had no colour and were always drawn with a pen. The addition of colour came after I studied colour at Arthur Findlay College in England. As I evolved intuitively, the mandalas did too.

My sister Jules was the first person to request a channelled healing mandala, and to this day, she still has that mandala in a safe place. During Jules's battle with an aggressive form of breast cancer, I continued to create healing mandalas for her. When one 'script' ran out, I would do another, as I mostly worked as a surrogate for Jules and channelled the healing directly to her.

I trust the spirit world and that what I channel will help those in need. All the intuitive work I do is a form of healing, and the mandalas are just another. Someone requested that I explain the meanings behind the symbols and colours on one occasion. I don't look that deeply; I trust in spirit and don't need to know how or why.

The Healer

There are always words of guidance that come with the mandalas, generally a few sentences, and what I call the 'prescription', or 'script'. The script is how the healing 'dose' of energy is to be administered—how often and for how long to get the total effect. I know that you cannot overdose on this form of healing.

I was recently asked to channel a healing mandala for a client's mother, who was rapidly declining in intensive care. Within two days of producing the mandala, the client contacted me to say that her mother was now talking in sentences and improving, an outcome that was not expected.

I in no way claim that the healing mandalas create miracles or cure anything or anybody. I have found that they do heal on some level, and there are always many layers of healing required at different times. Of course, if it is your destined time to leave this earth, I believe that no amount of healing can prevent that from occurring.

Why did I tell you this story? Because I believe that the more you develop your intuitive gifts, the more levels of healing you will be able to access. Intuitive people develop in many more ways than the traditional known ways as society changes and evolves. As I have developed, I have witnessed that I have been able to access higher levels of healing, and I have also seen this phenomenon among many other intuitives. I encourage you to keep developing in some way if you wish to increase your abilities.

Never underestimate your gifts, and be open to developing new ones. Sometimes your gifts develop in stages over time. You may not realise when you are learning a new skill or even understand the power that skill has.

Reiki

Throughout my life, I have studied many forms of healing. Initially, I didn't realise that I could tap into my natural healing powers, the ones I was born with, so I sought to learn many other forms of recognised healing.

First, I studied Reiki and became a Reiki master. I loved Reiki and the Reiki energy. I didn't research Reiki before I signed up and just thought I would go along to a class and that would be it, not realising that I would end up completing all the levels to become a Reiki master.

Traditionally there are three levels of Reiki, each building upon the other. The basic explanation below is what I was taught when I studied the 'Mikao Usui' method of Reiki. I have since discovered there are different variations on how Reiki is taught.

Reiki level one certification and attunement enables you to perform self-treatments. Daily Reiki self-care provides an opportunity to restore balance, reduce stress, anxiety and pain, and strengthen wellbeing. You can perform Reiki on yourself anytime and as much as you desire. This Reiki level can lead to an intense period of self-growth following your attunement.

Reiki level two certification and attunement enables you to perform distance Reiki techniques and become a Reiki practitioner. One of the benefits I love about Reiki is that when you give Reiki healing, you also receive Reiki healing at the same time.

Reiki level three certification and attunement allows you to teach Reiki and be known as a Reiki master.

I feel that learning Reiki helped to elevate my intuitive powers. It was like a key that opened the door for other intuitive gifts to develop further.

The Healer

Natural Healing

At the beginning of a reading, usually I psychically 'scan' the client's body and do what I call a health check. I will pick up any vitamins or minerals that could enhance their health or food intolerances, and I will feel any areas of pain they may have. I will become aware of their mental state and if they have reflux, toothache, arthritis and other symptoms. In many cases, I am mainly aware of health issues they already know about. How much I become aware of will depend on the connection to the client and if they are open to the connection. I have found that this is an excellent way to build the client's trust in my intuitive skills.

The Dark Shadow

In the early days of my development, I was sometimes startled by what I saw.

I never thought it would be possible to see illness in a person until I had the following experience.

Many years ago, a friend invited me to a workshop called 'Humans Becoming Better'.

The title didn't give much away as to the content, but she assured me it would be beneficial to both of us. While waiting for the workshop to commence, I glanced across the crowded room and was shocked by what I saw. Thinking it was an apparition, I quickly looked away and back several times, but it didn't disappear. I was looking at a lady with what appeared to be a murky black shadow covering the chest area of her body. As I focused on her, I suddenly felt overwhelmed, became emotional and had a sense of hopelessness as I inadvertently connected to her. I didn't realise that my reaction was evident until my concerned friend enquired if I was okay.

"Can you see that lady in the green dress across the room? I can see a black shadow in the area of her lungs, and I am feeling emotional about it. This has never happened to me before," I replied.

"Oh, Kathryn, I know her, and she has lung cancer," my friend sadly stated.

"Oh, no, that is so sad," I lamented, not knowing what else to say.

Apart from the shadow, the lady appeared healthy, but due to my reaction, I felt that this lady would not win her battle with cancer. Months later, while visiting my friend, she mentioned that the lady in the green dress had died and that she was going to attend her funeral.

I don't often have experiences like the one above, but I find it can be overwhelming when I do. I am confident that the spirit world is demonstrating another way that they can communicate with me. I would never tell someone they are going to die or diagnose any terminal medical issues, as that could get me in all sorts of trouble. It is essential always to have hope, as the brain is very powerful, and the wrong words can affect us in many ways. I recommend that you try to remain positive as much as you can, even in adverse situations, as it is believed that every thought has its own vibrational frequency. You want your thoughts to create positive experiences. Something that I realise is not always easy to do.

In this case, spirit made me aware that I could see more than dead people; I could see shadows and health issues in the here and now.

The Healer

Medical Intuitive

A medical intuitive is known as an alternative practitioner who uses their intuitive abilities to sense the health and well-being of others.

I don't claim to be a medical intuitive, but I can usually pick up anything I have already experienced or learned about.

For example, I once surprised myself and the client by asking her to confirm if she had Factor V Leiden. Whilst I could have stated, "I think you have Factor V Leiden thrombophilia," it would have then seemed that I was making a diagnosis, which I am not qualified to do and therefore would not do. I was even hesitant to ask the client to confirm something so specific in case I was wrong, and possibly the client may not have been diagnosed as yet. The only reason I could pick that fact up was that I have that blood clotting disorder.

Sometimes I see things that alarm me, and on one occasion, when I was scanning a client called Melissa, I saw dark cloudy areas around her abdomen, from her sternum downwards, and frankly, there was no way I was going to announce that to her. Can you imagine the fear I could instill in her if I told her what I was seeing? Instead, I mentioned that she felt very run-down, her energy felt low, and I asked her if she was experiencing any pain in her stomach. With that, Melissa confided that she had cancer in the area I mentioned and had been diagnosed as terminally ill. To anyone else looking at Melissa, they would have perceived that she was healthy. Melissa had come to me for healing.

"Melissa, I would be honoured to give you healing as long as you know that I don't profess to be able to cure anyone and that the healing will go to the areas where it is needed most," I softly stated. "I am happy to give you as much healing as you would like."

At the end of Melissa's reading, I commenced the healing that she had requested and decided to do a Reiki healing. Once that was completed, I felt compelled to switch to what I call 'natural' healing. I could feel the energy start to pulse through my hands, and after a minute, Melissa said, "The energy has changed; something feels different."

"Gosh, I didn't think you would notice. In what way does it feel different?" I enquired.

"At first, the healing felt warm wherever you placed your hands, and then the warmth stopped and changed to a tingly energy feeling that feels like it is radiating throughout my body," she explained.

I was surprised that Melissa felt the change in energy as I switched healing modalities.

As I continued the healing, I felt the energy grow stronger until it suddenly stopped. I then knew that the healing was complete.

Melissa continued to book in for healing, and towards the end of her life, her family would bring her to my cottage in a wheelchair. She did not expect me to cure her, although she hinted that a miracle would have been more than welcome. She would comment that she could feel a boost of energy after each session and felt more at peace with what she was going through.

I attended Melissa's funeral and was one of the last people to leave the service. As I went to the car park, a friend of Melissa's was trying to get her car started. I went over, introduced myself, and asked how I could help. She said her name was Beth (not her real name) and that she was a teacher and needed to get back to school. I agreed to give her a lift to her work, and she arranged for someone to pick up her car.

The Healer

As we were driving along and discussing how we both knew Melissa, Beth confided that she was very close to Melissa and that her death was hitting her hard. She was hoping that Melissa was finally at peace after her long illness. At that moment, the song 'Heaven Must Be There' by the Eurogliders started to play on the radio and I knew this was Melissa making contact and reassuring us that she was in a good place. The look of wonder on Beth's face was priceless; message received.

There are many healing modalities, and many of them work in different ways. The healing will go to where it is needed the most. If you are fated to receive a miracle, you will. Therefore, you should never give up. All healing is of value, and even more so if the intent is there. So never discount your healing abilities.

Healing From Spirit

Each time I attend Arthur Findlay College, I look forward to receiving a healing from the college healers that visit the college twice a week.

The healers work in a large, quiet, tranquil room that has a large amethyst cluster on display. On one occasion, when I went for healing, I was directed to sit in a chair in front of a young man who would stand behind me during the healing. I acknowledged him quietly, sat in the chair before him, and closed my eyes as he placed his hands on my shoulders.

I was enjoying the peace and tranquility, and after a few minutes, I felt an extra pair of hands on my body, and the energy grew intense. I was feeling hands in four different areas of my body. *Wow, two people are healing me,* I thought.

When the healing was complete, I opened my eyes to thank the people who had blessed me with healing, and I could only see the gentleman who had greeted me before my healing.

"Where is the other healer?" I whispered.

"What other healer? I am the only one who did your healing," he softly stated while looking confused.

"Oh, I thought that two people were healing me. I definitely felt two pairs of hands during that healing," I replied. Now I was the confused one. I looked around the room and saw a person sitting on every chair and a healer behind each chair. A few people were waiting for their turn to have a healing, so no spare healers were available. The gentleman guided me outside to question me further, as he could see the shock on my face.

"So, you say you felt two pairs of hands on you during the healing?" he queried.

"Most definitely. I am certain that two people were healing me. When the second person started healing me, the energy became intense," I replied.

"I was the only person healing you, and no one else was there. Interestingly, I have heard of a similar situation happening before, and that person was convinced that they felt two pairs of hands during the healing they received. I will suggest that you are truly blessed as it appears that spirit was also healing you."

I had requested healing, and with my permission, the spirit world had provided healing.

If you are open to receiving healing and request it, healing can occur. The law of 'free will' does not allow your spirit guides to intervene without your request.

Energy

I Married a 'Muggle'!

I married a muggle! What is a muggle, you ask? Obviously, I borrowed the term from the Harry Potter books. To me, a 'muggle' is someone who does not use their intuitive gifts, does not recognise that they have them or is a non-believer.

I mean, it is hard to believe some of the crazy stuff that happens in my life.

Tony and I have two beautiful adult children, but you already know that if you have read my other book. Our children have inherited intuitive gifts but choose not to use them professionally or publicly. When they were younger, to protect them, I encouraged them to 'fly under the radar', as I did at their age. At least until they understood their gifts and were strong enough to deal with repercussions. I have discovered that when people become aware of your abilities, they tend to have expectations that they want to be fulfilled.

Over the years, many strange occurrences have happened in our home—unexplainable situations. Things like electronics malfunctioning, lights flickering, TV channels changing by themselves, windscreen wipers continuing to work after the car is switched off and doors opening unaided are only some unexplainable situations I am referring to.

I often wondered if all these situations resulted from my energy, the spirit world trying to make contact, or just malfunctions. As your powers become more potent, it becomes easier to discern who is responsible. Once I got to the stage where I could work all that out, I then hoped that one day I could learn to control my energy better, and I soon found out that no one can control spirit energy. As for managing my energy, I am a work in progress and still working out the best way to live with the unexplainable. Imagine how it can be when you have more than one psychic in the house.

John has always channelled, and this shows in the amazing music he writes. Chloe is very tuned in, and not a lot gets past her. With three psychics in the family, it can sometimes be very challenging for Tony, although he is now used to all the weird things that happen around us.

Flickering Lights

Years ago, when John was a young teenager, we were sitting on the couch together, and John was explaining why his dad was upset with him and pleading his case. Tony then overheard us talking when he entered the room and became upset with John for going behind his back and coming to complain to me. He was also upset with me for defending John. Whatever the issue, I thought Tony was being too harsh on John, and he didn't have all the information. Everything we said at this stage seemed to inflame the situation further. We were both upset with Tony, and our emotional energy was building.

Energy

I looked at John to commiserate with him and grabbed his hand as Tony stormed away towards the laundry door, his voice increasing in volume as he ranted.

As Tony opened the laundry door, the ceiling light started flickering. He looked up at the light and quickly spun around to face us. Then as he glared at us, he yelled, "And you can both stop that shit right now."

"What? We're not doing anything," we said in unison as we looked at each other.

"I know what you are both doing; cut it out," Tony retaliated as he stormed off.

Then it dawned on me that Tony believed that John and I had made the laundry light start flickering.

"Mum, Dad thinks that we caused the light to flicker. Did we, and how did we do it? Why is the light flickering?" John asked.

"We didn't consciously do it. Maybe our combined energy affected the light because we are both upset," I replied.

It was also amazing that Tony blamed us, which meant he acknowledged our powers and thought we could cause the light to flicker. But did we do it? If we did, it was not intentional. I believe it was the energy we had produced, with both of us being upset simultaneously. We also had powerful allies in the spirit world. It looked like a situation that said, *"Don't mess with us."*

Most people would assume there was something wrong with the laundry light, but after years of witnessing all the strange occurrences, Tony had come to accept that this was how it was in our home.

In the early years of our marriage, the lights in our bedroom would sometimes flicker when I entered the room. Tony called in an electrician to fix the lights, only to be told there was nothing wrong with them. So, he accepted the flickering lights, and I figured out it was more likely to occur when my energy was intense.

The Lie Detector

In our current home, before we renovated the kitchen, we had a light that would randomly flicker; once again, an electrician was called in to fix the light but couldn't find a fault. After a while, I started to notice a pattern. The light appeared to flicker if someone was telling a lie or if something was not right. Now, I am not saying that anyone in the house was dishonest. I am sure anyone who has children knows that they are not always being truthful. The funny thing was that the light sometimes flickered when we had a visitor, and this proved beneficial on occasion and sometimes had us trying not to laugh. Unfortunately, when the kitchen was finally renovated, due to the changes made the light was removed—no more lie detector.

Everything is energy, and as you progress, protecting your energy and knowing what you can affect is essential. I know that after a full day of readings, it is important that I 'ground' myself before I touch any light switches, as I will either blow the light bulb or throw the power switch in the house, which then must be reset to regain power in the place.

Respecting your energy and learning to recognise how you may affect the energy in different environments and situations is essential.

Energy

Energy Upgrade

I always seek to experience the spiritual energy of different places during my travels while seeking to upgrade my intuitive powers. I have learned to look for the synchronicities, for signs that I am on the right path when seeking out some of these places. And I found out the hard way to ask for only what I can absorb and at the same time remain in good health. One such experience where I didn't add that proviso did not go so well for me.

I love visiting temples and will seek them out when travelling. I view temples as holy places that contain the energy of many who have prayed in them. On one occasion, Tony and I were on a cruise around Asia and docked in Hong Kong. We had been in Vietnam two days earlier, and it was swelteringly hot. But when we docked in Hong Kong, it was unbelievably cold. So unexpectedly cold that we were bused to a local shopping centre to purchase winter coats. It was said to be the coldest day in more than 50 years for that time of the year. Being 170cm (5ft7in) tall and long-limbed, the challenge was finding a coat with sleeves long enough, which proved impossible where we were.

Tony decided he was over the horrible weather and returned to the ship, but it was not enough to prevent my desire to visit a particular temple. Wearing a puffer jacket that didn't quite reach my knees, with sleeves that were inches too short, and an umbrella to keep me dry, I caught a taxi to the temple.

The temple was packed full of people bearing food offerings, and unknown to me, it was a special festive day. The only area anyone could access was not sheltered from the elements, and the smoke from the joss sticks and candles was incredibly cloying, stifling the air. While waiting in line to access the prayer area, where people were not packed so close together, I thought how much nicer it would be back on the ship with a lovely hot cup of cocoa.

Finally, I knelt in the prayer area, requested blessings for all my loved ones, and prayed for those in need. Then I asked for the highest spiritual energy upgrade that would enable me to develop my intuition and healing powers to extraordinary levels. I only meditated for a short while as others were waiting to avail themselves of the spot I was at. After saying the final prayers of gratitude, I left and headed back to the ship. The next day I was very ill and didn't have the strength to get out of bed.

Tony was worried. I had been bedridden for a couple of days, sick, weak and sleeping most of the time, while racked with guilt that I was wrecking our holiday. It is unusual for me to be that sick. On day three, I asked my guides why I was so ill after I had been to a temple, a healing place, and I was astounded by the answer.

Imagine you are a computer, and the energy upgrade is the software. The energy you asked for was so strong it was like trying to put modern software in an old computer. Your body was not prepared for it.

On the cruise, I had been indulging in food I usually wouldn't eat and burning the candle at both ends. I had not been looking after myself. My body was not prepared for such a high spiritual energy upgrade. It was like trying to update an iPhone 4 with iPhone 14 software; it would not be successful. At that time, I learned to always add the following provisos to my requests: '*if it is for my highest good*' and '*to remain healthy at the same time*'.

Energy

Your Energy Is Pushing Me Away

There is a beautiful place in Byron Bay's hinterland called the 'Crystal Castle' that is said to be built where ley lines (energy lines running along the earth) intersect. It is believed that where ley lines intersect, there are high points of energy or high concentrations of electrical charge.

At this special place, you can stand between what is said to be two of the tallest crystals on earth, walk along pathways lined with rose quartz, see the world's largest amethyst geode, find a 4-tonne mini mountain of rose quartz, walk the labyrinth, attune to the crystal spiral, and that is only mentioning a few of the highlights there.

On one of my visits to Crystal Castle with my friend Elly, I spent a couple of hours trying to take in as much as possible of this remarkable place. Elly patiently followed me and waited while I meditated in a 120-million-year-old amethyst geode. I had decided this was an excellent place to ask for a spiritual energy upgrade and was sure I would be guided to be in the right place at the right time for this to occur.

I could feel the heightened energy and was blissed out on it most of the time. As I vaguely wandered along a narrow path, I heard Elly get upset and say, "Stop it!"

I turned around and asked if she was okay, to which she replied, "You keep pushing me away every time I try to walk close to you; stop it." She was annoyed, but I couldn't work out why.

"No, I don't," I confusingly replied, not knowing what she was talking about.

"Yes, you do," she argued as she walked towards me. "Your energy keeps pushing me away."

Does she think that my energy keeps pushing her away, seriously? What on earth could be happening? I thought as I witnessed her being blocked. Then I realised I was going through a spiritual energy upgrade, and that explained why I was so 'spacey' and why the spirit world was keeping Elly away from me and out of the energy.

Now Elly is not a woo-woo person, and it seemed like she was starting to freak out just a little while she tried to process what was happening.

To defuse the situation, I replied. "Sorry, Elly, I didn't realise I was doing it."

"OMG, that is so weird; I can't believe that happened," she replied, looking at me strangely. Then I diverted her attention to the enormous rose quartz crystal we were walking towards.

Spiritual energy upgrades don't necessarily occur at the exact time of your request, with many occurring sometime after. It depends on your location at the time of the request, and it is possible that you may not be aware at the time that they are occurring. I have found that I am unconsciously guided to be in the right place at the right time to facilitate the energy upgrades if they are meant to be.

Uluru

Uluru (Ayers Rock) had been on my long wish list of places to visit for some time. So, when the opportunity to visit Darwin came up, I thought it would be good to just 'drop in' on the way home. Unfortunately, when I tried to book the trip, I discovered that Uluru is so not on the way to my home, and it would be an expensive diversion.

Energy

Then you could say that all the stars aligned to enable a trip to Uluru when I found discounted airfares and a special accommodation deal, including a field of lights tour. Suddenly Uluru was firmly in my future.

One of the main reasons I desired to go to Uluru was to experience the energy there. Uluru is known as the solar plexus chakra of the world and is said to connect to some amazing ley lines. I wanted to experience this magnificent rock and do some creative and spiritual work while basking in the incredible energy of Uluru.

Many synchronicities happened on my way to and at Uluru, so I felt positively excited about my visit. I won't go into all of them, but one was that when we were in Darwin, we checked into room 137 (in numerology this number adds up to 11). Then in Yulara we stayed in room 137. What are the chances of that happening?

Other signs demonstrated that I was on the right path, such as a heart-shaped rock in the middle of a trail (I was born on Valentine's day, so it is one of my symbols), and I kept seeing my spiritual empowerment symbol, a spiral. Many other signs and symbols along the way caught my attention, and the rock had an aura or an energy that was obvious.

One of the synchronicities that amazed me was a chance meeting. I had in my mind that I wanted to climb the rock, but I am very aware of my limitations due to having EDS (Ehlers Danlos Syndrome), a connective tissue disorder. I also didn't have suitable shoes for climbing the rock, which is known to have steep, slippery angles.

We arrived at the base of the rock, and after days of it being closed due to high winds, it was finally open to climbers. Once we got to the start of the incline, I could go no further as my feet kept slipping out from under me, and I could imagine that it was highly probable that I could do serious damage to myself.

I looked up and wondered *if I managed to climb further up, how will I get back down?* Tony, who was ahead of me, advised me not to do it, knowing how 'klutzy' I could be due to having hyper-mobility (part of EDS), which affects my balance and dexterity. It was time to admit defeat! I had come far enough; it would be an excellent place to meditate and connect to the rock's energy.

I sat quietly with my eyes closed and experienced waves of energy washing over me. After a while a young lady asked me if I was okay. I opened my eyes and reassured her that I was fine and had been meditating. We conversed, and she confided in me that she was physically limited as she had Ehlers Danlos Syndrome. Wow! What an unbelievable coincidence (between 1 in 20,000 to 40,000 of people are diagnosed with EDS). What were the chances? We got to compare notes on our lives with this syndrome and much more. She was happy to see someone much older than herself still living life actively, although with some limitations. Here was another synchronicity and a message that everything was as it was meant to be.

No Flies on Me

The next day we visited Kata Tjuta (the Olgas). Again, amazing energy, synchronicities and bothersome flies that were relentless; wearing a fly net was a sanity saver. Each time we got into our hire car, we were racing to beat the flies to ensure they didn't get in with us; unfortunately, we were rarely successful.

On one occasion, as we were driving along with annoying flies all around us, I decided to be a bit of a smart-ass for a laugh. I opened the car window on my side of the car and said gently, "Out you go, I have had enough." Tony looked at me incredulously as if to say, *"Don't be stupid, as if that is going to work."* To my utter surprise, all the flies on my side of the car went out the window and the only flies left were on his side of the vehicle, even though both windows were open. I then looked at Tony with a cheeky grin and asked, "Would you like me to get rid of your flies too?" Then I thought to myself, *how on earth did that happen?*

The beauty of Uluru and Kata Tjuta will stay with me forever, and so will the healing and lessons I learned there. It is said that Uluru is where indigenous men's secret business is done, while the nearby Kata Tjuta is a place for indigenous women's secret business. Yes, even here there is balance, and by visiting both sites, I ensured balance. I left Uluru feeling very blessed.

There are many spiritual energy spots around the world. To absorb the energy and receive a spiritual energy upgrade, all you need to do is ask and accept. Different types of energy from other sources will affect everyone differently depending on how much energy they can assimilate.

On a further note, did you know that when a celebrity or someone well known dies, you may feel sad even though you didn't know them, as it is possible that you could be connecting to the energy stream of those mourning the loss? For example, when Princess Diana died, millions of people mourned her tragic passing, people who didn't even know her or know why they were affected to the extent that they were.

Mercury in Retrograde Sure Packs a Punch

Have you ever heard someone curse or complain about the effects of Mercury in Retrograde? I know that I'm one of those people who often do. When Mercury enters the retrograde period, my life can turn into chaos. This astrological phenomenon is renowned for being responsible for many misfortunes, delays and misunderstandings.

Mercury is said to be retrograde when it appears that the planet slows down, stops and then goes backwards in its orbit as viewed from earth, all of which is an optical illusion.

Over the years, I have suffered and continue to be affected by the impact of the 'Mercury in Retrograde' (MIR), which seems to be worsening as time goes by. The MIR period occurs three to four times a year, each for five weeks, including both shadow periods (the week on either side). Some of the effects are said to include the following:

- Communication issues—misunderstandings and miscommunications; it is essential to watch what you say during this period
- Transportation and travel—delays and disruptions; it is best to allow extra time for wherever you are travelling to. Avoid buying any form of transportation like cars, boats and motorbikes
- Electronics and technology mishaps—don't purchase anything with electronics, including vehicles, phones and computers
- Contracts—avoid signing contracts
- Projects—don't start any new projects; it is better to finish off existing ones

To summarise, the way to survive Mercury in Retrograde is to choose your words wisely, avoid signing contracts, proofread everything very carefully, back up all data, reconfirm all your plans, and plan for travel delays and mishaps.

Considering the above, it is obvious why Mercury in Retrograde is a dreaded inconvenience. During the retrograde periods, I see many of my peers struggling. My logical husband constantly questions, "Why does it affect you so much, and why do we have to suffer the effects?" Yes, he said "we" as a lot of what happens to me affects him too. He now jokingly calls it 'Mercury in Reprobate', meaning roguish and unprincipled.

In the past, our flights have been delayed, our luggage lost, and on a recent stay in a hotel, the television would often turn itself off for no apparent reason, which was very annoying. Bookings have been lost, flights cancelled and recently, a trade show where I was working opened an hour later than the advertised time, and it just happened to be the first day of Mercury going into retrograde. Appointment times will be mixed up, delayed or postponed, timers will fail, traffic jams will occur, causing delays, and contracts signed during this time will often cause problems.

Mercury Is My Nemesis

I was over living in fear of the effects of MIR and planning my life around Mercury and its antics, so I consulted with my good friend Moira, who is deeply into Vedic astrology, as to how I could minimise the effects. Moira then recommended I consult with a highly revered astrology guru to find out how to sort out my problems with the planet Mercury. At the time, I laughingly thought, *I am going to a mediator to try and make peace with a planet; I must be crazy!*

The guru was a lovely, wise man and advised me that Mercury was sitting in a particular position on my natal chart. Therefore, Mercury was my enemy and always would be. After enquiring what I could do to lessen the effects, I was advised to wear peridots or emeralds during the MIR period, and so far, it has somewhat helped.

I have discovered that the MIR period often highlights any issues or problems, especially if something is defective. For example, if something is faulty, it is sure to fail during the MIR period to reflect that something is or was not right, and if there is a communication issue, it will be discovered. The following story recounts an example of Mercury at its finest.

Hello Lesbian ...

Something didn't feel right. I couldn't put my finger on what it was, but I felt ill at ease and unsettled. I had been communicating via text with a lovely lady in Europe named Leslina, who had heard about me and loved *The Modern Oracle* deck. Leslina was creating her own oracle deck, and a mutual friend mentioned that I would be able to advise her. After sending many messages back and forth, we finally found a time that suited us both.

It was now the day before we were due to meet via Skype, and I had a feeling that Leslina would not be able to make her appointment. Trusting my intuition, I decided I would send off a text to check if we would be connecting the next day. Due to being in different time zones, I knew it was possible that it could be many hours before I would receive a reply.

I was constantly yawning after an exhausting day and hastily sent Leslina a text before I dragged myself off to bed. I was hoping that she would receive my text during the night and that I would read her reply in the morning.

I lay down on the bed and found I couldn't sleep. I had an uneasy feeling that I couldn't shake, a feeling that something was not right. I started reviewing my day in my mind to try and discover the cause of this unease.

Check your phone ...
Check your phone ...

Energy

This thought was repeatedly running through my mind, and I knew I would get no rest until I checked my phone.

I went downstairs to my office, picked up my phone and saw that it was still open on the message I had previously sent to Leslina, and as I read the text message, my unease quickly skyrocketed to full-on anxiety. The ever-helpful spellcheck feature had changed one significant word in my message, and it now read …

'Hello Lesbian' …

OMG! Spellcheck has changed my text from 'Hello Leslina' to 'Hello Lesbian'.
OMG! What am I going to do?
I don't know how to retract this message.

In my panicked state, I could not think clearly. I decided that there was only one thing that I could do: send another message apologising profusely and pray. Before I hit send, I checked the message and discovered it had happened again.

'Hello Lesbian, I am so sorry that I called you a lesbian …'

Shit, shit, shit, it won't stop changing her name.

I typed Leslina again and then discovered the little 'x' that you click on to prevent spellcheck from changing the word. I wonder how many other messages I had sent incorrectly.

Tony thought it was hilarious. Through my inattentiveness and spellcheck, I had possibly labelled this lady something she wasn't, and he was laughing at me.

Eleven long hours later, I received the following reply …

'Hey Katy, no problem! It happens all the time when I sign off at the bottom of my emails!'

I imagined her signing off 'love Lesbian' instead of 'love Leslina' and the confusion it would cause; some may even think she was 'outing' herself.

My intuition was correct; Leslina needed to cancel her session with me due to a family crisis. When we finally did catch up, we had a good laugh, and she was so lovely about it.

"You know I will have to put this in my book," I said.

"Yeah, you can do that," she replied laughingly.

This experience reminded me of the importance of checking all communication, especially during the Mercury retrograde periods. I find the pre-shadow and post-shadow periods torment me as well.

It would be remiss of me to neglect to mention the positive benefits of Mercury in Retrograde. It is an excellent time to finish off any jobs or projects, find lost items, redo failed projects or things that need updating, and reconnect with people from your past. It also is an excellent time to do any of the following, and you will notice that they all start with 're'.

- Review
- Renew
- Recover
- Re-evaluate
- Restore
- Redo
- Reflect
- Retrace
- Remodel
- Repair
- Restructure
- Rest
- Reconsider
- Reassess
- Revive

Energy

- Redirect
- Rediscover
- Revisit
- Regenerate
- Reconnect
- Reinvent

Unfortunately, once you learn about the effects of Mercury in Retrograde, you become very aware of it, as it is difficult to ignore. The best way forward is to use the MIR season to 're-everything' and once it is finished it is time to create new goals.

Do Vision Boards Work?

A vision board can be used as a visual representation of your dreams and goals that you intend to manifest.

My very first vision board was created in less than an hour at a workshop that was not specifically about vision board creation. The attendees were invited to quickly draw a list of what they would like, if money was freely available, on large blank sheets of paper with coloured crayons.

When I returned home later that day, I folded up the paper and hid it in a drawer where it would not be discovered. I was embarrassed as the drawings appeared childish and I thought the list was excessive. I had been raised to never ask for anything and to be grateful for the little I did have. I did not believe that the list was achievable; if it were, it would surely take a lifetime to acquire.

A couple of years later, I found that sheet of paper and discovered that everything on the list had eventuated. I was shocked. How could this be? Did I make those wishes come true, or was it coincidental? Were those desires in my mind, and I unconsciously made choices that led to them being fulfilled? I could have assumed that was the answer, but the only problem with that theory was that I was not the only one involved. I never discussed this 'shopping list' with Tony, and he was unaware of the finer details in the drawings on my sheet of paper. Yet, Tony was the one who discovered the only two-storey house in the cul-de-sac that would become our home. I had drawn a two-storey house and even determined what the neighbourhood would look like in detail. There were details in that drawing that I saw in real life. I had included the landscape, the hills, the horses in a paddock a couple of hundred metres away and the nearby beach. Maybe that drawing was a psychic prediction. No matter what the answer is, in hindsight, I can now see that these were signs that I was on the right path.

The Right Path

I am often asked, "How did you develop to the level you're currently at?"

You could say I have been on this 'psychic' journey my whole life, going from one experience to the next and with each new experience came growth and development. I never really thought, *oooh, I think I have moved up a level* and was mostly unaware of how my intuitive powers unfolded and grew stronger as time passed, until they were tested.

With each new experience, my power and understanding grew. I questioned everything about the spirit world, saying *if this is so, then show me proof.* I need to believe that it is correct for me to be able to trust what I am learning. I need to trust that I am not in this on my own, as I don't seem to have any control over any of it. I want to learn how it all works and what I am capable of; I want confirmation of what I have to offer the world.

The desire to dive deep into the spiritual world is hard to ignore. The unexplainable synchronicities, the extraordinary experiences and the energy all are intriguing and draw you further into this amazing world. The more you venture into the 'woo-woo' world, the more it calls you; it can be highly addictive to some. You may find you crave being in the energy, the vibrancy and the feeling that all is right in your world.

As you progress along your spiritual path, the desire to learn more and confirm what you learned continues to grow. Synchronicities are one way of confirming that you are on the right path. When I look back, I see that many synchronicities confirmed what was meant to be and that I was indeed on the right path, or else why would they happen?

If you read my previous book, *The Modern Oracle – How to Tap Into Your Unique Psychic Powers,* you will know that my husband's parents and my parents celebrated the same wedding anniversary. I took that as a sign that Tony was meant to be in my life, and that is just one of the many synchronicities that connect the two of us.

I think it is no coincidence that Tim Abbot, one of the best tutors I had at Arthur Findlay College of Mediumship, celebrated the same birthday as my father. I always felt he was the right tutor for me, and that synchronicity confirmed it.

When I first met Tim, I remember thinking, *I wonder if that would be what my father would look like if he lived to this age,* as even his appearance reminded me of him. There was also this feeling of being in the right place at the right time. Tim influenced my development considerably, constantly pushing me to try new ways of connecting to spirit. One of the greatest compliments was when he arranged for me to teach a development group that visited the college weekly.

The Right Path

Apparently, it is unheard of to be permitted to tutor at the college without completing many of their teaching courses that can have you constantly at the college over a long period, which is not practical for me. Not many people have the time and money to devote all their time to pursuing this vocation, especially when they live on the other side of the globe. When you do the tutor training at the college, there is no time to do anything else, it is costly, and most of us must work for the funds to pay for the training.

I feel that I muddled along as I progressed on the spiritual path, taking the apparent opportunities as they appeared and looking for even more. I kept moving forward, learning along the way with a compelling passion and desire. I learned the purpose of each new skill, and with repetition, my confidence grew, and so did my trust in each newfound skill and the spirit world.

Did the Earth Move for You?

On my first trip to England to attend Arthur Findlay College, you could say the earth shook. After travelling for 36 hours, I finally arrived at Heathrow Airport jet-lagged and was met by my now good friends, Alan and Sue. I had never met them before; they were relatives of my friend Dawn. Dawn had arranged for them to look after me as it was my first solo trip to England; frankly, it was exciting but scary too. I was so far away from my family that I would not be able to return quickly if needed. Tony was also feeling the same way; with me so far away and not knowing anyone, it would be difficult if anything untoward happened. My mother was concerned for a totally different reason; she thought I was going off to join a cult and had tried to talk me out of the trip several times. Anyway, it was a massive step for me to make this trip alone.

The Modern Oracle II

Alan and Sue were very hospitable hosts, and upon meeting them for the first time, I felt very comfortable. They had travelled nearly two hours to pick me up from Heathrow Airport, and now, on the return trip, I was jet-lagged and fighting to keep my eyes open. It was the end of February and oh, so cold.

It was decided that it would probably be best for me to stay awake until at least 9 p.m. if I was to have any chance of sleeping through the night. My body clock needed resetting to prepare for the long days at college, and I had planned a couple of 'jet-lag' recovery days so I would not disgrace myself and fall asleep in class.

After a lovely hot meal, I went to bed only to be awakened in the middle of the night by the bed being shaken. *What on earth could be happening, and why would anyone shake my bed like this? What have I gotten myself into?* These were my first thoughts as I awoke from an exhausted sleep. It was around one o'clock in the morning, and an earthquake that measured 5.4 on the Richter scale was occurring. As I looked around, the room seemed to sway. Earthquakes were not common in Peterborough and especially ones that strong. It was my first time experiencing an earthquake of that magnitude, so it was hard to go back to sleep, and I lay in bed waiting to see what else would happen. The following day there were jokes about how my arrival in England had made the earth shake. Welcome to England!

I spent the next couple of days having a fun time exploring some of the tourist highlights with my very hospitable hosts. Saturday came quickly, and it was soon time to set off on the 90-minute car ride to Stansted, where Arthur Findlay College is located. One of the trip's highlights was stopping at a lovely old English pub for lunch. I discovered that I was quickly falling in love with old pubs and their counter meals, and Beef and Guinness pie with its flaky pastry soon became my favourite meal to order. It hit the right spot in the cold weather, and I always seemed hungry. Sadly, it was disappointing to discover that many of the old pubs were closing permanently at a fast rate due to the changing times.

As we arrived at the college, I started to feel anxious as I thought about how I would be here on my own, and my insecurities about being good enough to be at the college were racing through my mind.

I was impressed by the magnificent old building set amongst ancient trees and beautiful gardens; this would be my home for the next two weeks.

Alan and Sue, not being 'woo-woo' people, were unsure what I was getting myself into. We all laughed when Alan offered to turn up with a ladder and help me escape if I didn't like college or if it wasn't what I was expecting.

Anyway, I loved college and went on to return many times over the next decade or so. I found it hard to stay away. It was like it was in my blood and calling to me, and I was always eager to return. As soon as I returned home, I would book more courses at the college and try to find the courage to tell Tony I was going back to England on my own. Every return trip to college included catching up and spending time with my now dear friends, Alan and Sue. It was as if we had known each other forever.

The two weeks at college seemed to pass quickly. I struggled through the first intense week of mediumship, and by the end of that week, I was left with an ongoing headache. I went from not knowing how to rate what level of skill I was at to "you must come back for the advanced class later in the year". Whereas the first week solely focused on mediumship and platform mediumship, the second week was a treat, and we focused on everything psychic. I had two excellent tutors teaching me many psychic skills and tools—think tarot, reading bowls of water or sand, learning about colour and auras, different ways to perform psychic readings and so much more.

I had also grown to enjoy the somewhat compulsory 30 minutes in silence, meditating each day. During the first week, the tutor watched that the class did not even twitch, let alone move, and if you didn't attend, you had to have a good reason. At first, I was restless and didn't think I had it in me not to get bored, but by day three, I had gotten into meditating and truly loved the feeling of being connected. I left college, promising myself that I would now meditate in silence for 30 minutes every day. Yeah, right; who was I kidding? Meditating in silence is challenging with two boisterous teenagers and dogs that want to sit on my lap every time I sit down.

I was sad to leave college and all my new friends that I had made, but it was time to set off on another adventure. One that I had secretly planned. I was going to Glastonbury.

Finding the Right Path—We All Want a Shortcut

Glastonbury had been on my bucket list for some time, and I had heard about the amazing 'vibe' there. It was supposedly a place that new-age people liked to visit. After much research, I found that the only way and the cheapest option on a Saturday was to travel by train to Castle Carey from Stansted and then take a cab for the 15.5-mile journey from the station to Glastonbury. This was going to be a big adventure for me, and I had secretly conveniently made all the arrangements and booked a B&B before I left Australia.

The B&B was lovely, and I was thrilled with my selection as it was just a random choice based on my intuition and my budget. I had not told

The Right Path

Tony I was doing this extra travel as I knew he would worry about me, and money was tight. I was notably vague about my travel plans, and he assumed I would continue on to London when I completed my time at college.

I was shown to the 'Citrine' room, aptly named as there was a large citrine cluster underneath a side table holding the kettle and cups. Other rooms were named after different crystals, i.e. the Amethyst room and the Rose Quartz room, and I could only assume that they, too, contained the appropriate crystal to suit the name.

The small room I was to stay in was decorated in yellow and orange 'Laura Ashley'-style floral wallpaper. The big bed (two single beds pushed together) took up most of the room, and I could see the Glastonbury Tor from the bay windows. The Glastonbury Tor is a hill near Glastonbury topped by the 14th century roofless St. Michael's Tower that can be seen for miles. This famous landmark is known as one of the most spiritual sites.

As I looked at the Tor through the drizzling rain, I decided I should climb to the top immediately in case the weather was worse tomorrow as I only had a few days to see as much as I could before I had to travel back to London. Remember, this was a sneaky trip that I had not declared to Tony so I couldn't hang about too long.

I found the owner of the B&B in the large kitchen and enquired about the easiest way to get to the Tor. The lady explained that, conveniently, there was a side road behind the house that led to the base of the Tor, and therefore I would not have to walk into town to access the path. She assured me that from there it would be easy to find the path that led to the top. Hmmm, she did not know about my lousy sense of direction. I had no map, and there was no such thing as a smartphone with google maps at that time. Tony often tells people that I have no sense of direction and that the only place I don't get lost is in a shopping centre.

I set off on my journey with an umbrella which soon proved useless in the drizzling rain and wind, and all I had was a woollen coat that was inadequate protection. I arrived at the base of the Tor, and the only path I could find was muddy and looked like it would suit mountain goats, not tourists.

I thought this must be it, or maybe it would lead to the right path as I started to follow the track. I walked for a long time, slipping and sliding in the mud, seeming to go nowhere fast, and I was getting drenched. *Surely this can't be the path everyone uses to climb to the top of the Tor. It feels like I could be going in circles, as I don't seem to be climbing any higher. Wait a minute; I remember that tree and its raised roots in the middle of the track.* Now I was sure I had already walked on this path. I was going around in a big loop.

At that point, I decided to take a shortcut and climb vertically up to the next track and get off this loop I was currently on, only to find that this track was no better and didn't lead up the hill. Once again, I scrambled up vertically to a higher track, holding on to the vegetation to prevent me from sliding back down, and then finally, I came across a concrete path that ended up being the right path to travel on to the top of the Tor.

Later that evening, while meditating beside the citrine cluster in my warm room, I realised that the walk up the Tor symbolised my spiritual journey to date. A challenging path that was taking me nowhere fast with many diversions as I continued searching for the 'fast track' and the path of least resistance. This was a turning point for me, a catalyst. No more rambling along; I wanted to take the direct route and help others to do so too. I was ready for change.

The Right Path

My 'Pot' Smoking Tour Guide

The next day I went on a tour that would take me sightseeing to Stonehenge, Avebury and the surrounding areas. When I booked this tour, I was clueless and found that there were not many options for tours out of Glastonbury, as most tours were returning trips from other cities, not Glastonbury.

My quirky tour guide Jill arrived in a small old car that had seen better days, with her cute but smelly dog sitting on the front seat. She announced that I was the only passenger as others had cancelled last minute, and she invited me to sit in the front seat as she chased the dog onto the back seat.

"I hope you don't mind if my dog Paddy comes along with us as I don't like to leave him home alone," she stated.

Paddy was a medium-sized terrier with a big personality. Being a dog lover, I didn't mind at all. That was until he jumped from the back seat to the front seat, landing on my lap. *Great, now I will smell like a wet, muddy dog.* After two weeks with no washing machine and limited clothes, I was wearing my only clean pair of jeans and was hoping to get more than one wear out of them.

"Aww, he really likes you," Jill happily stated. "He usually sits on the front seat; you don't mind, do you?"

Not wanting to take a chance that I could be left in the rain on the side of the road because I upset her dog, I replied, "Of course not, it's fine by me." It was obvious it was going to be a battle to get Paddy to give up the front seat, and it would probably be a bad start to the day if I rejected her dog and chose to sit in the back seat.

The Modern Oracle II

Jill was a lovely local artist who did these tours on the side for extra income. She was an excellent, caring guide and very chatty. She mentioned that her tour business had been a bit quiet lately, and she also confided that the previous night, she had drunk too much red wine, smoked too much pot and got it 'on' with a man she had recently met.

It was an enjoyable day even though, once again, it was bitterly cold and drizzling rain. So cold that the rain on my glasses kept icing up, and due to the relentless rain, Paddy was getting muddier each time he got out of the car. He had no intention of ever sitting in the back seat.

Towards the end of the tour, Jill asked if I would like to see a couple of ancient oak trees that were more than 2,000 years old, named Gog and Magog. They were known as the Avalon Oaks and said to be part of a Druidic Avenue of oak trees linked to the druids and pagan Celts and a place of pilgrimage for many visitors. Jill warned me that the road was too muddy to drive on, and we would have to traipse through the mud for the last couple of hundred metres on a farm road.

We set off in the cold with Jill chatting along as we slowly navigated the muddy, wet road looking for grassy spots to walk on. Suddenly, Jill's non-stop chatter ceased. Thinking something could be wrong, or I was going the wrong way, I looked behind to check on her. Bad mistake! Yes, she was still behind me, but I would never have expected to see her squatted in the middle of the road, in plain sight, relieving her bladder. Could the day get any more bizarre?

I quickly spun around and kept walking ahead before she could become aware that I had noticed what she was doing. Nothing was mentioned, and Jill was soon once again chattering away as we made our way to the ancient oak trees. When we arrived at the trees, sadly, it was evident that Gog was no longer living, with the remains of this

The Right Path

ancient oak tree still standing beside Magog, and we joked about how it is common for women to outlive men.

We were soon back on the road to my B&B, and my pot-smoking tour guide had no qualms in expressing her desire to get warm and enjoy another joint in front of her fireplace. As soon as she discovered I was a psychic, she thought it was okay to discuss her little 'habit' and regale me with her life story. This made me wonder why my being psychic would cause her to think she was in a confessional and that it would be okay for me to hear that she was pleasantly high when I got in her car this morning. Then I thought … *OMG, Tony will be so upset if he ever discovers that I was so trusting, but also not surprised that I was oblivious to her state.* I was now glad that I had refused the cookies she kept offering me throughout the day, as who knows what could have been in them.

It was a fun day, and I was happy that I trusted my intuition and ended up on a private tour with an unconventional tour guide. This whole trip had been one of me trusting my intuition and trusting that I would be in the right place at the right time and on the right path.

Your spiritual journey may never go to plan and don't expect a direct route to your goal. There will be many twists and turns in the path, and when you look back, you will find that you learned a lot along the way and made many connections. Trust your intuition and trust that you will be guided to the right path for you.

'Hogwarts'

That Table Can Walk!

On my second week at Arthur Findlay College, I was blessed to have Mavis Pittilla and Thelma Francis as my tutors. Mavis is known as 'AFC royalty', as she has worked with the spirit world for over 50 years and was trained under the watchful eye of her friend and mentor, Gordon Higginson, who is known as one of the best mediums that the UK had ever seen in the 20th century. Over the years, Mavis has trained many high-profile mediums from around the globe. Thelma Francis is an amazing tutor and medium from Scotland who loves to work with colour. At the time of booking my courses, this was all unknown to me; there was hardly any information on the internet, and my choice of courses was determined by the dates that I could get away from work. Fortunately, I ended up being on one of the best courses with two amazing tutors.

One evening, I was introduced to and participated in 'table tipping'. The announcement that our class would experience a séance and

The Modern Oracle II

table tipping with Mavis Pittilla excited the students who knew of Mavis. For those who don't know what table tipping is, the definition, according to the Merriam-Webster dictionary, is as follows: *the lifting or manipulation of a table during a séance attributed to the agency of spirits.*

The excitement was contagious, and all the students were encouraged to examine the room where the séance was taking place before starting. We checked that none of the devices that were going to be used had any wires, fishing line or anything that could make an object float or move unassisted. The four-legged cane table was scrutinised very carefully. Usually, a three-legged table is preferred as it is deemed to be easier to get moving, but, in this instance, they didn't have one.

There also was a trumpet: *a cone or horn-shaped speaking tube that were said to magnify the whispered voices of spirits to audible range*— according to Wikipedia. This trumpet had fluorescent tape wrapped around it that was clearly visible in the darkened room. For safety reasons, the room was not entirely dark, only dimmed, and we could see each other and would notice if anything untoward happened.

With the lights dimmed, the music commenced, and we all started to build the energy in the way we had been instructed to do. We relentlessly worked on building the energy, and nothing was happening. *Oh no,* I thought; *I hope this will not be a flop.*

A gentleman called Richard had his music system there and was the composer of the beautiful meditative music being played.

After a while, with still no result, it was decided that the music was not uplifting enough to build the necessary energy. Other types of music were also played to no avail. Then it was suggested that we sing old war songs, e.g. 'The White Cliffs of Dover' and 'We'll Meet Again'. All songs that I didn't know very well. Maybe these old songs would

'Hogwarts'

appeal to the spirits of the convalescing soldiers from war times, and hopefully, they would come out to 'play'.

The singing got louder, and after a few minutes, the trumpet slowly started to levitate off the table it was sitting on. The trumpet would drop back down onto the table whenever we stopped singing. We quickly ran out of songs everyone knew the words to, so we kept repeating the same ones. There was no playlist; someone would just start singing the song with everyone else joining in quickly.

After a while, we then moved on to 'table tipping'. Four students were invited to place two fingers from each hand on each side of the tabletop. Everyone else was encouraged to keep singing, knowing that we were all going to get to experience the table moving.

I had my fingers on the table as it suddenly started rocking back and forth and slowly rocked across the room. It was becoming challenging to keep our fingers on the table to keep the energy flowing and, at the same time, stay out of the table's way as it changed direction.

Then amazingly, the table slowly rocked up the couple of stairs that led to the podium, paused and then descended and continued to rock across the room. When the table paused, the tutors would exchange the people at the table while mindful that some students appeared to not have the same effect on the table. It was amazing to experience the energy in the room.

Go Away!

I had often wondered if just anyone could go to Arthur Findlay College of Mediumship. I mean, you are not screened before you attend; you book the course that interests you and turn up. I wondered what would happen if someone unsuitable attended the college. The following story answered my question.

The college sometimes attracts people that are not suitable to be there. On the night of the séance, there was one such lady. She stood out in the crowd because she stated she was a witch and dressed accordingly. She had designed her long, dark-coloured cotton dresses with two small 'U' shaped pockets in line with her ankles on either side of the dress. She told everyone that these dresses were big sellers, and she couldn't keep up with the demand for them. Many of us started to think something was not quite right with her, and she seemed very eccentric. Obviously, the pockets would be decorative only as most contents would fall out as you move. Not to be judgemental, but many commented that she seemed a little crazy. She also struggled to do the class content.

While we were conducting the 'table tipping', as the table started moving in her direction, much to my shock, she was hissing "f**k off" repeatedly and shooing the table away with her hands. There was a weird expression on her face, and it wasn't fear. I was not the only one to notice her behaviour; the next day, she was asked to leave the college. Well, that answered my question about if just anyone could attend the college. Yes, you might be there, but that doesn't mean you get to stay. It would also be very challenging if you could not do the set work.

That was another thing that I pondered. Had anyone been asked to leave if they were not a good fit? I had noticed that the ones who couldn't do the work would often say they were sick and hide in their room or skip class. In one of my courses, they offered to call a doctor for a student who didn't attend class because she said she was unwell. Miraculously she turned up to the next lesson in good health. The next day, she left the college due to a family emergency.

In all the classes at the college, you are expected to participate. Many of them require you to connect to a spirit known to the recipient and deliver accurate evidence for their loved one. This is very nerve-racking for some, and it soon becomes apparent who can achieve this, who can't and who could be attempting to work at the wrong level. It is expensive to attend college, leading me to assume that only the keen and gifted would consider undertaking a course. Many of us, like myself, end up at Arthur Findlay College because we want to learn how to get the best out of our intuitive gifts, become aware of other intuitive gifts and work on advancing spiritually.

Do Your Intuitive Gifts Deteriorate With Age?

During the first few years I attended the college, I often noticed a well-dressed elderly lady who looked to be in her 80s. I had heard that she was a good medium and was at college a lot, but sadly her intuitive gift was seen to deteriorate in her advancing years, and she would sometimes fall asleep during the lectures.

That was something else that I had pondered. Do your intuitive gifts deteriorate when you become elderly, as your body does? From what I have observed, it does for some. It depends on your mental state as you age and if you desire to continue working as a medium. We all age at different rates and can have various health issues; some look after their bodies better than others. This all influences your performance in your later years. Some people become more fatigued when they work and don't have the same stamina they did when they were younger. This is the same for most people. When you are younger, you can run faster and further without injury. In later years people struggle to maintain the same fitness levels.

Around retirement age, many psychics choose to retire or work less, just like anyone in any other profession.

Seeing the elderly lady at college prompted me to think, *How cool would it be to attend college in your latter years? I imagine that if you could afford to, it would be fun to sit around receiving readings all day, mixing with younger people and not have to do much more. Your meals are all provided, and your room is cleaned.* To my way of thinking, if you are well enough, it would be better than sitting in a nursing home all day.

Can the Spirit World Interfere With Your Electronics?

I can honestly say that I have experienced Arthur Findlay College in all seasons. I have attended courses at different times of the year, and let me tell you that summer in the UK at times feels like winter in Hervey Bay. I think my favourite time to visit is in April when all the daffodils are in bloom.

One of the joys of attending college is walking around the beautiful gardens and long walks to the nearby village during my breaks while taking in the lush landscape of green fields and different wildlife. Each time I walked to the village, there was something new to see. Walking was my main form of exercise while at college, and it was when I had time to clear my head, de-stress and re-energise. Sometimes a new friend would ask to walk with me, and we would explore the nearby church surrounded by tombstones or visit the nearby horses in the paddock.

I looked forward to mealtimes and eagerly waited for the daily menu to be posted on the dining room door. College food was generally very good, but how enticing it could be really did depend on the chef at the time of each visit. During my first visit, the food was really enjoyable and later in the year, for my second visit, it was very much a case of *What the hell happened? How can they get it so wrong, and let's go get a pub meal in the village?*

In the early years of attending college, everyone was served the same big hearty meals delivered to your table in the dining room. Everyone was expected to sit in the same seat at the same table for every meal so the waitstaff could find you in case you had special dietary needs. You couldn't change your meal if you didn't like what was served as they didn't prepare extra meals. After a few years, the college changed the meals to buffet style, and you would point out what you would like to be added to your plate.

In my first year of college, I went over in April and then again in November, and both of those times, I returned home with three extra kilos of excess baggage on my body. Regretfully, I indulged in the lovely hot desserts served with lunch and dinner. These delicious desserts were very hard to say no to.

I could have chosen to eat less, but where is the fun in that? I have a sweet tooth, and I looked forward to the meals they served, and I was determined to indulge in the whole college experience. The cold weather made me hungry, and the classes were long and sometimes stressful as I anxiously waited for my turn to do the current exercise, which always put me out of my element, and comfort eating helped ease my stress.

On the November trip, the days were shorter, and it constantly rained, which meant that exercising outside was not an option. After mostly sitting down all day, I felt the need to burn energy, and on wet days, I would dance in my room to music on my iPod; yeah, it was that long ago when iPods were the most advanced technology. Luckily, I was staying in a single room and would not be bothering anyone as I pranced around in the small room.

The Modern Oracle II

My iPod contained the latest top 40 music and many dance tunes. I was set. I went to my room during the lunch break, put the earbuds in my ears and started dancing. I was having a good time and getting more aerobic exercise than my walks provided. The third song came on and only played for a few seconds, then stopped. I was confused. Why would my iPod stop like that? The battery was fully charged, and my iPod was only a couple of months old. I unsuccessfully tried everything I could to get my iPod to work and then assumed it was faulty. I was not looking forward to the long flight home without it.

That night, I was sitting quietly on my bed, typing out my notes from my classes, when I heard in my head, *"We don't like your music."* I stopped what I was doing and thought, *Did I imagine that?*

I continued typing and heard again, *"We don't like your music."*

Now I knew I did not imagine it. Then I recalled what I had learned earlier that day about how Stansted Hall was loaned to the Ministry of Defence in the Second World War for use as a convalescent hospital by the Red Cross. During this period, some 5,500 soldiers, recovering from accidents, wounds and illness, recuperated within its walls and enjoyed the beautiful surroundings. Many people had died in the place, and it was definitely haunted.

The other information that came to mind was how I witnessed during a 'table tipping' exercise earlier in the week that the spirits of the hall preferred old war tunes, and I guessed that the ghosts in my room were objecting to my music.

Each day I tried to get my iPod to work to no avail. A couple of days later, the sun finally came out, and I could go for a long walk around the gardens. As I walked, I decided to try bargaining with the energy that had stopped my iPod from working. I said aloud in the middle of the garden, *"If I promise not to play my music in my room, will you please give me the use of my iPod back?"*

I didn't hear a reply, but I did feel a sense of peace. I finished my walk and went back to class.

That night I once again tried my iPod, and it worked. Unbelievable! They had let me have the use of my iPod again. I was so happy as I feared it would never work again. Since then, I have always kept my promise and only played my music when outside of the Hall. I was in their territory and needed to respect their wishes.

The spirit world is all around you; sometimes, it can be necessary to find a way to live with them and their preferences and always show respect.

Connecting Via a Chair

As I have mentioned before, I was pushed out of my comfort zone whenever I attended Arthur Findlay College and pushed into doing what I thought impossible, and with that, I grew stronger each time.

During one particular class, instead of the usual circle of chairs for the students to sit on, there was one row of chairs facing the back of one vacant chair. An empty chair usually suggested that whoever was chosen to sit in that chair would be the one connecting to spirit.

Uh oh, we must be going to do something new, I thought. *I hope I don't have to sit in that chair. Maybe if I don't make eye contact, I won't be chosen to go first.*

"For this exercise, one of you will leave the room while another will sit on this chair for a minute and then return to your seat. The student outside the room will be called back in and invited to sit on that chair, face the wall with their back to the rest of us, and do a reading for whoever previously sat on it. The rest of you will sit quietly, and I will be the only voice that will respond to the reader so that there are no clues as to whom they are reading for," the tutor explained.

Gosh, is that even possible? I thought. *Hmm ... I hope so.*

The chosen student to be the reader left the room, and quietly the tutor pointed at another student who would receive the reading to silently sit in the chair and then indicated for her to return to her seat. The student outside the class was invited back in, sat on the chair, and proceeded to do the reading. Most struggled as it was just not their strength, and some connected to a different person in the room and not the intended recipient, which was disappointing and not what the exercise intended.

We all hoped to receive messages and proof of survival from our loved ones in the spirit world, and of course, the reader wanted to do the exercise correctly and make a connection. Then there were the few that nailed it and provided accurate evidence for the correct person whose residual energy was on the chair from when they briefly sat on it.

After half the students had had their turn, it was my turn. I now believe it is less stressful to go first and do the exercise so you can then relax, because by this time, my anxiety had ratcheted up.

"Kathryn, can you please leave the room? It is your turn to be the reader," the tutor requested.

I slowly left my chair, and as I suspected, you could not hear anything once outside the room. After a few minutes, the door opened again, and I was invited back in. I sat on the chair and waited for something to

'Hogwarts'

happen. I thought I would feel something, and I didn't. Then suddenly information started to pour into my head slowly, and I began to deliver the evidence to the class. Like every other time, only the tutor's voice could be heard speaking on behalf of the intended recipient, who would silently nod or shake their head, and the tutor would respond accordingly. The evidence started to get personal as the recipient's loved one divulged information about her extensive collection and love of shoes, and much more. I kept stating the information and gathering more upon request. Then in my mind, I saw the tutor's face.

Hmm … what is that about? Why would I see her face when we are supposed to be reading for one of the other students? I thought. The image of the tutor would not go away.

"Do you have any idea who sat in the chair before you?" the tutor asked.

"Well, I was expecting the connection to be for a student, as per the exercise, but your grandmother in spirit is telling me the connection was for you," I advised the tutor. There was a long, uncomfortable silence.

"Yes, it was me. I sat in the chair. I wasn't trying to trick you; I just wanted you to see what you were capable of as you would not have expected it to be me," she stated. "I don't know why you are always surprised by what you do. You should have more confidence in your abilities."

I immediately once again thought, *OMG, I did it, and I wonder if I can do that again?* I was relieved and happy, and then my next thought was, *Thank God I have had my turn and don't have to do it again.*

Why did I think that? Well, the tutor was correct; I did not have confidence in my abilities. Being a type 'A' personality and a perfectionist, I like to be in control, and when working with the spirit world, you can't control anything. Therefore, I find it all very stressful.

Tony often says, "Don't put so much pressure on yourself and continue to do this work if it stresses you out."

But I always think I was given this gift for a reason, and what I do can be a form of healing for many. Bringing messages and assurance from loved ones can comfort those grieving or missing their loved ones in spirit.

You don't know what you can do until you try. The more you do something, the more confident you will become, and even though you may not control your gift, it is still worthwhile taking a risk and getting out of your comfort zone. With trust comes confidence.

I Want a Medrado!

The students at college were all excited. As they all busily chatted, you could feel the elevated energy. It had just been announced that we were about to witness something extraordinary. Later that day, the very talented trance medium Jose Medrado (known as Medrado) would demonstrate his gift of painting whilst in a trance.

First, we had a lecture from Medrado on what to expect and the conditions he liked to work in while he was in the trance state, including the expected behaviour of everyone attending. He informed us that he would be doing a channelling demonstration, allowing the 'Masters' to paint through him on canvas with acrylic paints and mainly using his fingers (not a brush).

At the end of the demonstration, the paintings would be auctioned off, with all proceeds going to the orphanage he founded in Brazil.

He shared with us that when the 'Masters' first approached him about channelling their art through him, there were conditions and that he

'Hogwarts'

believed they would not work for him if it were for his own personal gain. It was a requirement that all proceeds from the art go directly to the orphanage he had established in Brazil.

The time came for all the students to watch Medrado work, and you could feel the energy in the air change as he went into a trance. The music he liked to work to boomed out of the speakers, and a camera closely filmed all the action for those who could not get a seat close enough.

Set up in front of Medrado were many palettes of paint, a different one for each of the famous painters who worked through him. Each time he started working with another artist, he would change the paint palette to suit that artist. He mostly painted with his eyes closed, and each painting took between 9 and 12 minutes to create. I could feel the energy in the air as his hands quickly flew across the canvas. It did not seem possible that he could keep adding thick layers of different colours without them bleeding into each other. I know that when I have applied wet paint onto wet paint, the result is usually a muddy mess.

I watched as his paintings astoundingly came to life in minutes. In front of my eyes, Medrado was channelling many famous artists, such as Van Gogh, Picasso, Renoir, Monet and many others, all working through him. It is remarkable to see and experience how beautiful paintings with healing energy are created within a short time.

I decided that I wanted a 'Medrado'. Nearly everyone in the audience wished to acquire one. During the short break, the audience chatted about how unique his channelled paintings were and what a gift it would be to own one. Many who had previously acquired a painting by Medrado stated that the artwork evolved over time, that they were healing and indeed something extraordinary to acquire. Everyone viewed the paintings, with many deciding which ones they would bid on.

The Modern Oracle II

By now, I was caught up in the hype and was thinking about the logistics of getting a painting home all the way from England to Australia on a long-haul flight and the many other forms of transport before the flight. I would be leaving the college the next day on a train with a heavy suitcase and hand luggage, and I was unsure how long it would take for the thick layers of paint to dry completely.

When the auction started, the first painting went relatively cheaply. Then as each painting was sold, the prices continued to rise steeply. The final painting had been bought for thousands of pounds. Well out of my budget.

A couple of years later, I discovered that Medrado was coming to Australia, but by the time I found out, it was too late for me to travel so far on short notice. Medrado was being hosted by a lovely friend who suggested that she could represent me and I could bid over the phone, which I gratefully accepted. I was not particular about who the channelled master was, or which painting I purchased.

The time of the auction arrived, and I excitedly waited for the phone call from my friend. I knew from experience that the best strategy would be to buy one of the first paintings being auctioned before the prices increased, and I was praying that I would be successful.

Luckily for me, there was a small audience that seemed to have a small budget, so I was able to purchase the first two paintings that were auctioned. Excitingly, I now had my very own Medrados and planned to collect them on my next trip to Sydney.

As I unwrapped the paintings, the energy emitting from them was noticeable, and I have since seen slight changes within the paintings. Depending on the angle and how hard you look, you can see faces and animals that are not part of the intended artwork.

'Hogwarts'

When Tony first saw the paintings, he looked at me as if to say, "What are we going to do with these?" After I explained the paintings' significance, he was happy to hang them on the wall. Now when we get visitors, he is sure to let them know that one of the paintings was painted in only nine minutes. Mind-blowing!

If you believe that you will be able to manifest your desires, it can happen when the time is right and if it is meant to be.

Messages and Visitations

Sometimes the Shower Can Get Crowded

Often, when I have a shower, I will receive messages from the spirit world. For me, the shower is like a portal to the spirit world where I can obtain information. But of course, it is not practical to do readings from the shower; now, that would be awkward.

When Chloe was 10 years old, I would drive her to a nearby town every Saturday to learn how to embroider from a lovely lady called Adele. As it was a bit of a journey to get to her house, I would wait while Chloe had her lesson, and after a few weeks, Adele invited me to start an embroidery project to fill my time while waiting. I soon became addicted to embroidering beautiful projects, and Chloe and I would eagerly look forward to our mother-daughter time each Saturday. All was going well until Adele became unwell, and disappointedly, classes were cancelled until further notice.

The Modern Oracle II

One evening while in the shower, thoughts of Adele and her situation popped into my mind, and I knew that I had to check on her and suggest that she might like to make an appointment to see Kate, a naturopath I had great faith in. Kate was very dedicated to her job and had a busy practice.

From conversations I had overhead while attending Adele's classes, I was sure she did not believe in psychics or alternative medicine. I knew I would have to be very cautious with my recommendations. The next day I visited Adele.

"Adele, how are you feeling?" I softly enquired.

It was evident from looking at her that she was unwell, and as I sat across from her, I found I could feel all her ailments.

"I feel so sick all the time. I have been to many doctors, and none of them can diagnose what is wrong with me. I think that they think I am a hypochondriac. I don't know what else to do or who else I can see. I want to be well again," she ranted.

I then thought I would describe all the symptoms I was now feeling and ask if she was feeling that way. As I vocalised them to her, she agreed that she felt each one as I described them. She now had an incredulous look on her face.

"How do you know all that?" she asked.

"Oh, I have a friend who had the same symptoms," I lied (really, it was just a little white lie). I mean, there was no other way I could get the point across to her and be taken seriously.

Messages and Visitations

"What did the doctors find wrong with her, and is she well now?" Adele hopefully enquired.

"Oh, she saw this amazing naturopath who comes highly recommended. You might like to try her as you say you have run out of other options," I answered and gave her Kate's details.

A few weeks later, sewing lessons were back on, and Adele could not speak more highly of Kate. She had diagnosed and treated Adele successfully.

Ooh, I Think She Can Hear Me

Imagine that you are in the spirit world, and you keep trying to get a message through to your loved ones, and it is just not happening. You can see how frustrating it could be. That is why the spirit world will take any opportunity to get their messages through.

Another shower connection occurred when my good friend Marilla's mother, Betty, who had sadly died when Marilla was in her 20s, contacted me and appeared holding the beautiful baby blanket she had handmade for my babies. She knew I would meet with Marilla in the next few days and was taking the opportunity to communicate beforehand.

Betty wanted me to give the baby blanket to Marilla now that my children had outgrown it. She regretted that she hadn't gotten around to making a blanket for Marilla and knew I would understand. I was happy to pass on the special blanket as I knew Marilla would be grateful. Yes, the blanket had sentimental value to me, but I knew it would be even more special to Marilla, who appreciated the gesture.

Do You Know When He Is Going to Die?

One of my clients once asked me if I could tell her how much longer her beloved father had to live and if he would die anytime soon. She had accepted that he was dying and had taken time off work to care for and be with him in his final days. Her concern was that she was running out of annual leave and was soon expected to return to work. As a single mother, she needed to keep earning an income to pay her bills and support her family.

"I am sorry, Sarah; I have asked never to see when someone is going to die," I said.

Long ago, I had communicated to the spirit world that it was not information I wanted to know. I didn't want to be the 'scary' psychic that could predict when someone would die. I could see no reason to deliver such upsetting news.

A couple of weeks later, I was taking a shower before breakfast and suddenly felt a presence, followed by a glimpse of an older gentleman's face. Upon asking who he was, the gentleman explained that he was Sarah's father (I had never met him before) and that he had died that day. He wanted me to reassure Sarah that he was fine and to thank her for looking after him so well. Then he went on to inform me of other information Sarah would want to know.

I raced out of the shower and quickly wrapped a towel around me on the way to look for a pen and paper. I needed to write down the information he was now relaying before I forgot it. As I was writing and dripping water everywhere, Tony appeared and looked at me as if I was crazy.

"What are you doing? Can you hurry up? I thought you were getting ready to go to breakfast. Can you do whatever you are doing later? You

Messages and Visitations

don't want to miss the breakfast cut-off time," he stated impatiently. Time was running out before the hotel buffet would be closed.

"I have to write down these details before I forget them," I replied as I scribbled away.

Not wanting to keep Tony waiting any longer, I quickly dressed and went to breakfast. As I started eating, Sarah's father appeared again; he had more to say.

Two days later, I received a phone call from Sarah.

"Hello, Katy, I am sorry to bother you," she started to say before I interrupted her with the following.

"Hi, Sarah, did your father die on Wednesday?"

"Yes, that is why I am calling. I thought you would want to know. How did you find out?" she quietly enquired.

"He visited me in the shower and let me know he had died on Wednesday," I answered. I then continued to pass on his message.

"Katy, I am sorry that Dad interrupted your shower; I was calling you to let you know he had died. I appreciate you passing on his messages; you have brought me peace of mind. Can you please tell Dad I love him?" she requested.

"He already knows that, and you can tell him yourself as he is with you and will hear you," I quietly reassured her before ending the call.

Naked Conversations

I am sometimes asked if it concerns me that I am naked while talking to those who are no longer living, and my answer is always that they are not interested in my body parts; they are only interested in communicating.

Once when I mentioned to a client that her mum is always with her, she became a little distressed and replied, "She's not watching me have sex, is she?"

"No, she has better things to do. Your loved ones are not interested in that part of your life, and no, they are not watching you go to the toilet. Believe me, that is another subject I am often asked about," I laughingly replied.

Hauntings

Can the Spirit World Warn You If Something Is Not Right?

A beautiful heritage-listed hotel in the middle of the Brisbane CBD is over a hundred years old and is haunted. Every time I have stayed there, I have experienced some form of paranormal activity.

The first time Tony and I stayed in this hotel was so that we could check out an apartment that was for sale. I suggested that we stay there for a night to experience what we could potentially invest in.

This particular hotel has an old-world feel and has been remodelled to reflect the era it was built in. It is situated in a great location with restaurants and shops nearby; this hotel always seems busy and is often booked out.

After checking in at the hotel reception, we went to find our allocated room. As we walked along the corridors, it felt like we were stepping back in time, and I loved the 12ft ceilings. Even though I could feel that this place was haunted, I was looking forward to a comfortable stay and was hopeful that I would not be haunted. I have noticed that the spirit world likes to take any opportunity to connect, especially if they know you can communicate with them.

That night we went to bed only to awaken a few hours later, feeling like we were sleeping in a refrigerator.

"Tony, are you awake?" I asked. "It feels so cold; I think we need another blanket."

"I'll go and adjust the air conditioner and warm the room up, and there aren't any more blankets," Tony replied. He then turned on a light switch and checked the wall's old-style air conditioner control switch.

"No wonder we are cold; the air conditioner is switched down as far as it can go," he stated.

"I didn't do it. You know I don't like the cold," I replied.

"Well, it is on the lowest temperature setting, and it wasn't like that before we went to bed. The dial can't just change on its own," he stated as he looked at me.

"As if I would turn it down to freezing," I replied sarcastically.

After resetting the air conditioner, Tony returned to bed, only for it to happen again a couple of hours later.

"What the hell is going on?" he asked. "It is impossible for the air conditioner temperature dial to keep turning down." It was the early morning hours, and we were both tired and cold, and the air conditioner was again on the lowest setting. Tony reset it once again and returned to bed.

The next minute a loud droning noise started, and it sounded like it was coming from outside our window. We looked out the window and discovered the noise came from a compressor unit a few floors below.

"What else can go wrong?" Tony grumpily asked. "I can't believe this," he added while looking for an extra pillow to place over his ears to block the noise. It seemed we were not going to get much sleep.

"Tony, I feel that we are not meant to buy this apartment. For whatever reason, we are being warned off. It is so haunted; I don't know that we would get much peace when I am here," I said.

Then, suddenly the engine noise stopped. There was the confirmation of what I had just said. For the spirit world to intervene meant that this apartment was unsuitable for us to invest in.

That didn't stop us from returning as Tony loved the charm of the old building, and clearly, he forgot about the sleepless night.

The Territorial Ghost

Our next visit to this hotel was months later. We planned to meet up with friends in the city and had booked a room to stay in overnight. Even though it was not the same room, I could still feel a presence. We went out and had a good time with our friends, and later that night, Tony decided to continue socialising after our friends had left, and as I was tired, I returned to our room. I instantly felt a change in energy as I entered our room, and something didn't seem right, but I was too exhausted to get my head around it; I had a shower and went to bed.

The Modern Oracle II

Later that night, I was awoken by the sound of the door opening, and I felt a cold draught on my face. With the bed far from the door, I knew it wasn't the door opening that caused the draught. I peeked through my eyelashes to see Tony entering the room and thought, *I am glad he is back safe,* before I closed my eyes to continue sleeping.

A few minutes later, I could hear Tony conversing with someone, but he was doing all the talking. *Who the hell could he be talking to?* I wondered and opened my eyes to see him talking to a spirit, which was why it was a one-way conversation.

"You say this is your room, and you were here first?" Then there was a pause in the conversation, and Tony added, "That's okay, you can still sleep here too. I will move Kathryn to make some room so we can all fit."

Then Tony started gently manoeuvring me across to the edge of the bed. I could smell the rum reeking out of him and decided to play possum because he was well beyond getting any sense out of and I was curious to see what would happen next.

OMG! I couldn't believe it. Tony was talking to a somewhat territorial ghost (spirit). He then patted the middle of the bed and told the ghost there was room for him too, then flopped down on the bed, fully clothed on the edge of the opposite side, and promptly started 'drunk' snoring. Tony didn't know that the ghost had died while staying in this room a long time ago.

The following day, I awoke to find Tony asleep, fully clothed and still at the very edge of the bed, and the heavy energy was gone. Upon waking with a slight hangover, he had no recollection of the events from the night before and found it hard to believe that he had conversed with a ghost in his inebriated state.

The Upgrade

The next visit was with our children. We rented a two-bedroom apartment, so everyone had a bed. My mother was staying in town and came to visit and check the place out before we all went out to dine.

I had also received a phone call from our niece, saying she would be in Brisbane and wanted to spend time with us. We invited her to join us as she hadn't yet booked anywhere to stay. We planned for her to sleep on one of the two single beds, and our teenage son John would sleep on the couch. Even though it was going to be a tight fit, John was so easy-going he didn't mind giving up his bed for his cousin. I also knew that he loved falling asleep in front of the television.

"Did you know this place is haunted?" my mother asked.

"Definitely," I replied and proceeded to inform her about our previous stay in this hotel.

"Are you worried about it?" she asked.

"No, not really," I replied.

A little later, I went into the main bedroom and found that the curtains were still pulled closed from when Tony had a nap earlier. As I pulled the curtain open, the large, heavy wooden curtain rod fell from the top of the 12-foot wall and grazed the side of my wrist as it brushed past me and landed on the floor with a loud thud. I let out a yelp, and everyone came running into the room to see what had happened. Luckily, I had only sustained a bruised wrist. I thought, *how on earth did that happen?*

Everyone settled down, and I phoned reception to report the incident. They found it hard to believe and expressed that there was no way that the curtain rod could fall for no reason as they were engineered to hold over 100kg.

"Did you swing on the curtain?" the receptionist enquired while trying to shift the blame to me.

"No, I just tried to pull the curtains open. I am not in the habit of swinging on any curtains, and I only weigh 68kg, so it shouldn't be an issue," I replied. "If you can't put the curtain rod back in place, then we will need to move to another apartment, as we prefer privacy."

We were moved to the only other apartment available, which happened to be the penthouse apartment on the top floor—a much bigger apartment with more bedrooms that would accommodate us all comfortably.

The next day when I was checking out of our accommodation, the receptionist commented that it was just as well it didn't happen to the next family that were booked in to stay in that apartment, as they had young children, and it would not have been good if the rod had landed on one of them.

After thinking about what had happened, I concluded that the curtain rod falling at that time highlighted that there was a problem and probably saved a life. That thick wooden curtain rod could undoubtedly do some damage if it fell on you.

The Face in the Mirror

After dinner, John and I returned to the penthouse apartment, and he went to the bathroom. I had just settled in front of the television when I heard John scream. I rushed to the bathroom and called through the locked door.

"John, are you okay? What has happened? Are you hurt? Can you let me in?" I questioned loudly. He threw the door open, and I swear his face was as white as a sheet.

"Mum, I was washing my hands and looked into the mirror and saw a face staring back at me. Make it go away. I can't take anymore." John has been able to see spirits since he was a child; this time, the unexpected visit frightened him.

"John, I am sorry this has happened to you. You know that this place is haunted," I soothingly replied.

"I am over it, Mum. I have no privacy! How do I stop it?" John exclaimed.

"Honey, you know that spirits will take any chance they can if they are aware that you can communicate with them," I gently stated.

"It is not fair that they frighten me like that. How do I get it to stop? It is just not right," he protested.

"Okay, John, I will have a word with them and ask for you to be left alone," I reassured.

Luckily, John was left alone for the rest of the visit. After mentioning the episode to Tony, we decided not to bring the family to this hotel again. In fact, to date, we haven't stayed there since.

The first time I experienced paranormal activity at that hotel, I thought it was just a one-off. The second time I thought it was a coincidence and maybe just particular to the room we stayed in. The third time was the last, as I prefer a good night's sleep and an incident-free stay.

Don't let my experiences put you off staying there, as it is a lovely place. I am sure most people who visit there would not have to worry about being haunted; when I say haunted, I don't mean a horror movie experience.

I have discovered that there are many reasons the spirit world will attempt to communicate with you, especially if they are trying to warn or protect you or draw your attention to something they want you to notice.

Readings

Why Do People Visit Psychics?

Most people who request a reading are searching for guidance or a connection to one or more loved ones in spirit. Some seek advice and reassurance that everything will be okay or better and that they will survive their current situation and get what they desire.

When I created *The Modern Oracle* deck, I knew that the deck had to apply to as many aspects of life that people would seek guidance for so that this could be a relevant tool to enrich a reading. Calling on decades of experience as a professional psychic, I narrowed it down to six topics people request guidance about. I will discuss them below in no particular order.

The first area and the most prevalent one is **relationships**.

People have different relationships with friends, family, partners, children and even animals. Relationships always seem to come down to love, respect, desire and connection. Some of the questions that people will want answers to are as follows:

- Is this person the right one for me?
- Is my partner cheating on me?
- When will I get married?
- When will I meet the love of my life?
- Will my child/parent/partner ever forgive me?
- Will I be able to fall pregnant?
- Am I having a boy or a girl?

I am sure you are starting to get the picture with the few examples I have listed above. Generally, people are searching for a connection or guidance through their various life stages.

I want people to understand that our lives are forever changing, and our actions can determine the outcome. At the time of your reading, I can see your current path and give you guidance that can lead you in the best possible direction. Then it is all up to you. I can't hold your hand to keep you on the desired path to create the best outcome, and each detour can lead you off track.

For example, a victim of domestic violence may be going through the worst challenges in their life, but they will stay on the same path until they are ready to make changes. In the sitting, it may come up that they are best to move on from their physically or mentally abusive relationship, but they choose not to. They decide to stay on the same path they're on with the hope that it will improve or stop, and of course, it doesn't.

The second most prevalent topic people seek guidance for is their **health**.

Readings

Usually, people will ask about their health when they can't get answers from medical professionals or have been told there is no hope of a cure or recovery. Generally, psychics are their last resort. I choose not to diagnose health issues as I am not a medical professional. Usually, if something comes up about their health during a reading, the client is already aware of the symptom or condition, and I am made aware of it to confirm my accuracy and build their trust in my ability. It can be common for clairsentients to feel the aches and pains that their clients are experiencing.

The third topic that clients may enquire about is their **careers, work or studies** with questions like the following:

- Will I get a promotion?
- Will I get a pay rise?
- Will I get a job or the job I have applied for?
- Will I pass my exams?

The fourth topic they may enquire about is their **finances and investments** with questions like the following:

- Will I be able to afford my own home?
- Should I buy an investment property or a particular property?
- Will I have enough money to retire on?
- When will my house sell?
- When will my financial situation improve?

The fifth topic they may enquire about is **travel** with questions such as:

- Will I travel overseas?
- Will I be safe on my holiday?

The sixth topic that they may enquire about is **spirituality,** with questions like the following:

- Who is my spirit guide?
- Am I on the right path?
- How can I progress more quickly?
- What are my intuitive gifts?
- Will I ever be able to do professional readings?
- Why can't I meditate?
- How do I know if I am a medium?
- How come I can't feel the presence of spirit?

Can All Psychics Communicate With Your Loved Ones in Spirit?

People also seek to have a reading because they want to have a 'family reunion' with their loved ones who have passed over to the spirit world. Psychic mediums are known to have the ability to communicate with the spirits of the deceased.

According to Wikipedia, *Mediumship is the practice of purportedly mediating communication between familiar spirits or spirits of the dead and living human beings.*

Most of you can imagine or know how sad it is to lose a loved one and being able to make contact with them can assist with the grieving process. Maybe you didn't get to say goodbye or want to know that they are okay. These are just a couple of reasons a client may wish to have a mediumship reading, which can prove that the spirit lives on.

Readings

Over the years, I have connected many people with their loved ones in spirit. More often than not, these readings are very sad and can leave me feeling shattered by the suffering of those mourning tragedies.

I have seen a grown man cry as I connected him to his beloved dog in spirit. He had arrived with the dog's favourite toys in a bag and did not mention them until after the reading. He brought them along to ensure that his pet would be there.

For many clients contacting their loved ones can help them to keep going when they are enshrouded with grief. Then some want to ask for forgiveness so they can release feelings of guilt for whatever reason, most of which are generally unfounded.

Whatever the reason someone may wish to connect to their loved one, to do so, they need to see a psychic medium. Not all psychics have the gift of mediumship and many who do usually discover that there is a family connection somewhere in the gene pool. Maybe a parent or a great-aunt was a medium. Some mediums cannot trace whom they inherited their gift from because it was not discussed or was kept hidden in previous generations.

Why Do You Want to Hang Out With Dead People?

I shied away from mediumship readings for a while as it was getting me down. One day Tony asked me, "Why do you want to hang around with dead people when you can be with the living? You will get to join them soon enough." He had a point.

Then a few days later, I talked to one of my peers, and she confided that she had given up doing mediumship readings because it was too draining and depressing. She, too, thought she would rather live life than spend most days talking to the dead. I thought there was a clear message and decided to have a break from mediumship.

Not long later, when I was doing a psychic reading, I was aware of the client's deceased husband. As much as I wanted to ignore him, I couldn't be that disrespectful. So, I passed on his message, and the joy that message brought to his wife made my job worthwhile.

It is always sad when connecting a parent to a deceased child. I genuinely believe that it is cruel to outlive your children. Recently I did a reading that 'haunted' me for days. It was so sad that I couldn't stop thinking about it. I usually don't remember much about the readings unless they shock or surprise me or are emotionally haunting. The following is an extract from my journal, and it should give you an idea of why mediumship is not glamorous but can be rewarding.

Today, I did a reading that has emotionally haunted me. I can't get the reading out of my head, and I have been left feeling the devastation that the client was feeling.

No sooner had I greeted the client and explained what I do, I felt the energy change. The feeling quickly intensified to what I can only describe as a wall of grief.

I was looking at the client, a lovely lady in her 40s, and immediately felt overwhelmed. Even though she was not expressing any emotion, all I could see was sadness and pain when I looked into her eyes.

I wondered how she was keeping it all together and remaining so calm as the sadness kept intensifying, and I felt seconds away from tears as the sadness encompassed me.

"Did you receive the photo I emailed you?" she quietly enquired.

Readings

People send me photos of those they wish me to connect to: the living and the deceased. It is another way I can connect.

"I am sure I have; let me go and find it," I replied as I opened my iPad and searched through my incoming emails, using the time to centre myself.

I found her photo of a young teenage girl, and the connection was immediate as I looked at her image. I felt her grief, and I could feel her spirit near me. I knew that this reading was going to be an emotional one.

The young girl, her daughter, had hung herself at the very young age of 16. Her father had found her lifeless body and immediately tried to resuscitate her to no avail. I can't begin to imagine how he felt at that moment as he tried to breathe life back into his beautiful daughter. I am sure it included a feeling of helplessness, along with panic, shock and pain.

Her mother could not understand why her happy, well-loved young daughter would commit suicide. She certainly appeared happy when she had last seen her the morning of that day. The young girl said she was sorry, regretted what she had done and wanted to return. She missed her parents and could see the repercussions of her actions. How distraught they were and how many lives she had affected.

She was this lady's only child, well-loved and popular. She had many friends and a lovely boyfriend. She wanted to let her parents know that she was safe. She had changed her mind just before she took her last breath, but it was too late. It wasn't their fault; nothing they had done or hadn't done would have influenced her actions. As I held back the tears, I brought through information and messages about the lovely young lady to enable the healing process to proceed.

The mother wanted to know why and what led her daughter to do something so drastic and continued to ask her daughter questions. "You know I love you; why did you do it? How can I go on without you? I miss you so much. Is there anything you want me to know? Everyone is upset and sad."

I know I have been trained not to show emotion, not to cry, but I am an empath, and I was taking on the feelings of both the mother and the child. I don't know how this reading could not have affected any medium. When you are truly connected, you get to experience all the emotions.

I wept after the call had finished and wondered if I would be able to do the next reading, which was due to commence in the next 10 minutes. I had to pull myself together as the next person, in all reality, had probably been waiting months for their reading with me. They now needed my whole-hearted attention. I took a few deep breaths, wiped my face, drank water and connected to the next client on Zoom. It is what I do. I hoped it was a psychic reading where I was dealing with everyday problems and not as emotionally draining.

When Tony came home, I unloaded to him without mentioning names, not that he would know them anyway. That evening I went to Zumba to de-stress and dance my cares away. To release any pent-up energy. On the way there, I called my beautiful daughter Chloe and felt grateful that I still had that opportunity. Chloe, being a trained psychologist, was very healing to talk to.

"Mum, you offer these people something they cannot get from a psychologist or a doctor. You are amazing!"

Gosh, I am so blessed to have Chloe.

I went to bed still thinking of that reading; it had affected me that deeply. The following day Tony complained about the battery-operated light on the stairs going on and off randomly all night and how he took the batteries *out to disable it. He then jokingly asked if I was bringing my work home again, and I gave the usual reply that it was not intentional. We were being haunted, something that we are both used to.*

I have found mediumship readings can be draining, and I try to limit the amount I do each day and consistently seek to recharge my energy at the end of the day. Being in nature or walking on the beach and breathing in the sea air is my favourite way to recharge.

Can You Not Do That Thing You Do?

Tony and I had been invited to dinner with someone he was thinking of working with and he wanted my opinion. He was eager to make a good impression and wanted us to appear 'normal', or I should say, for me to appear 'normal' as I met him for the first time.

As we drove to the restaurant, Tony commented on how nice this guy seemed (whom we will call Mark, for the point of the exercise).

"I would like you to check him out and tell me what you think of him. I think he is a good person, and I hope to learn a lot from him," Tony said.

"Okay," I replied. I was not looking forward to this evening while they discussed work, but it was important to Tony.

"I am sure you will enjoy his company," he added, "but can you not do that thing you do, and if you do, don't let him know you are doing it."

"Okay, I won't embarrass you," I replied. I knew what 'that thing I do' meant.

The Modern Oracle II

Sometimes if I felt compelled to, I would scan people and then offer guidance through the conversation we were currently having and, at the same time, lead them to believe that the source of information was the knowledge that they had already imparted to me.

"I'm not saying you embarrass me; it is just that not everyone understands or believes in what you believe in," he replied while he quickly tried to smooth things over so as not to hurt my feelings.

"I am sure we can find many other things to talk about," I replied.

The evening was going well, and Mark was a lovely man. Then halfway through the meal, I saw an older lady in spirit standing behind him. It was his grandmother. *Oh no!* I thought, *she wants to communicate, and I'm not allowed to!* So, I smiled and tried to ignore her. The more I ignored her, the more insistent she became. She was determined to communicate with her grandson and was not going away.

As Tony and Mark discussed different subjects, Mark's grandmother would let me know her opinion on the matter. So, I did what I did when I used to hide my gift and somehow tried to put the advice into the conversation. It didn't take long for Tony to become aware of what I was doing. He then gave me an annoyed look that said, *"Stop it!"* But it was too late; my cover was blown.

Mark looked at me strangely and asked, "How did you know that? I don't think I have mentioned that before, and no one else knows about what you just said." Busted.

At this point, Tony gave up and replied, "Oh, she is a bit psycho, I mean psychic!" This was his joking way of explaining the unexplainable. With that, Tony arose from his chair, annoyed, and said, "I am going to get a drink." Then glared at me and added, "Don't make him cry."

Readings

Mark looked at me curiously and asked, "What is he talking about?"

"Well, um, sometimes I know things," I replied, not giving much away.

"What sort of things? Are you a mind reader?" he asked jokingly.

"No, I can communicate with people who have passed on to the spirit world." This appeared to be the easiest way to explain what I was doing.

I now had his attention, and Mark proceeded to question me further. He wanted to know how I was receiving the information that I seemed to know, that I couldn't possibly know. He then excitedly confirmed that he was very open to discovering more and believed in what I was doing.

When I think about it, I am sure his grandmother would not have come through in such a public place if he was a non-believer.

His grandmother communicated to me mainly via images (clairvoyantly) and sometimes hearing (clairaudience). I saw pictures that appeared to be like a movie on a super 8 film (with stuttering between each frame) of Mark's childhood memories. As I went into more detail, he started to cry quietly. The tears were running down his face, and he was scrambling for a napkin.

"I watched that super 8 movie for the first time the other day," he stated as he wiped away more tears. "What you have described is what I saw in that movie."

I continued to pass on all the information his grandmother wanted him to know, and Mark was very appreciative and encouraging, not wanting the connection to end.

Tony was very considerate and gave us a bit of privacy while I was passing on all the messages, and when he finally returned to our table, he took one look at Mark and then me and said, "Did you have to make him cry?"

"It's all good, mate; it really is all good," Mark confirmed.

We went on to enjoy a lovely meal with Mark, still somewhat shocked but excited about hearing from his much-loved grandmother.

Mediumship is a wonderful way to connect to your loved ones in the spirit world, and it can be a very healing experience where your loved ones can come through to communicate with you for many reasons, from letting you know they are still with you, that they love you or even to apologise and set things right.

I have learned that the spirits generally don't present themselves if they feel their recipient is not open to receiving their messages.

There Is a Tool for That

Do psychics receive warnings before any negative situations or impending problems?

Mostly, there is a warning, but I don't always recognise it or the signs until after the situation because I am preoccupied or distracted and remain oblivious.

I have found it essential to learn how to communicate better with your 'spirit team' in whatever way is best for you. Communicating with your spirit team can be like learning another language, where you learn to recognise signs and symbols and how to communicate differently.

Readings

One of the reasons I channelled *The Modern Oracle* decks was to have an accurate tool to use to 'read' for myself and anyone I am close to and can't objectively read for.

Sometimes when I am demonstrating the accuracy of *The Modern Oracle* decks, I have heard the comment, "Oh, I don't need cards to do a reading."

Tools are not necessary to do a reading but using the right tool that you trust can undoubtedly enhance the experience. Just like building a fence with a nail gun would be quicker than using a hammer, think of *The Modern Oracle* deck as the nail gun for a faster, easier reading that requires less energy from the psychic.

Can Psychics Get It Wrong?

When a psychic gets it wrong, it is usually because they didn't listen to their intuition or there was a lesson that was destined to be learned. It can also be that they were influenced by outside factors and emotions that have the potential to taint their interpretation of the information they receive and, therefore, possibly lead to adverse outcomes. Some clients will even badger the psychic until the psychic agrees with them, even though it is not their perception of the subject.

A psychic offers guidance to assist you in determining the best path and direction for you moving forward. It is always your decision about your actions and whether you heed their advice or stay on your current path. A bit like when a doctor advises a patient to quit smoking to improve their health, and they don't because they don't want to, or it is too hard for them to do so. If they were to cease smoking, they would have an opportunity to head in a healthier direction and possibly a different future.

Each psychic has strengths; most of the time, it can depend on their own experiences. If you have no knowledge or are unaware of the existence of something, then it is unlikely that you can receive comprehensive information about it. I know I won't be aware of a name if I have never heard of it before. Like anything, the more experience someone has, the greater the chance of accuracy. I might see an image of a car using my clairvoyance, and then I have to work out the issue with the vehicle. Is it a new car, money spent on a car or a road trip? When using my clairvoyance, a picture really can paint a thousand words, and it is a bit like playing charades; you have to work out what it is all about, and we all know how easy it is to get it wrong in that game.

You should also be aware that psychics can get the timing wrong, as your actions can also determine the timing. I always say the spirit world has no need to measure time; therefore, I don't rely on them to predict the timing.

Is It Difficult to Read for Sceptics?

I find it harder to read for sceptics as they are closed off. They emit an energy that is like a barrier that prevents me from connecting to them, and their scepticism is off-putting. Many sceptics will not entertain anything outside their beliefs and will negate anything you say, even if it is accurate. This has the potential to bring your energy down and deplete your confidence. It is essential to value your time and not waste it on anyone who does not believe in what you do.

Challenges

'Psychic Amnesia'

Excuse Me; I Don't Remember You

One potential pitfall when you are a medium is that your client may sometimes have 'psychic amnesia'.

Psychic amnesia can rob you of your confidence. Anytime your client answers "no", there is the potential for your confidence levels to drop. Once your confidence levels drop, so does the trust in your connection to the spirit world or the source of information.

Unfortunately, some clients forget their family in spirit, or they may not know everyone on the branches of their family tree. They could be adopted, or their family tree was never discussed. There are many reasons why the client might be unable to identify the spirit you are communicating with. This is when doubt can come in, and it is easy to doubt the accuracy of the medium. I recall that one of my clients did not realise that her grandmother's name was Anne because she was always referred to as Granny and died when the client was a young child.

The other challenge can be that the client hopes to connect to a specific person, and when other friends or family come through who they haven't thought of, they then fail to recognise them, as they were not their immediate focus. Usually, the spirit they want to connect to will come through, but they may not be the first to show up.

Sometimes the client will forget information, such as names, dates and events. I once had a spirit bring through a memory that the client could not relate to, and then when they looked back through a photo album, there was evidence of that memory.

The Forgotten Sailor
A recently widowed lady called Veronica came to see me wanting to connect to her beloved husband, Fred. The reading went well until I mentioned that Fred was showing me images of the ocean and boats. Information that she could not relate to.

"Did your husband like to sail or go out on boats?" I questioned while trying to jog her memory.

"No, he didn't do that," was her reply.

I still saw the ocean and boats, and the images would not go away. I needed to solve this puzzle as her husband was being persistent. A challenge I sometimes encounter when using my clairvoyance (clear seeing) as I have to determine what they are trying to say by showing me a particular image.

"Do you know if he had anything to do with boats?" I further questioned as I thought, *where is he going with this, and why am I just not getting it?*

Challenges

Once again, her answer was "no".

"Well, I will leave it with you and maybe you might recall something later."

Ten minutes later, once again, Fred showed me the boats. I thought *I can't mention that again as it was getting me nowhere,* and I tried to ignore the image.

As the reading progressed, other information was brought through that delighted Veronica, and she made comments like, "That is exactly what my Fred would say."

Then as we got to the end of the reading, much to my relief, Veronica happened to mention that her husband was in the navy for years and was always on boats!

What Do I Do If I Don't Understand the Images I Receive?

Before I had an office, I used to travel to the sitter's (the recipient of the reading) home to do their reading. Tony and I decided that we would like to preserve our privacy, and it wasn't always convenient to have people coming to our house, especially if our children were home or we had visitors. Going to strangers' homes was not ideal and was very short-lived. I was losing time having to travel as well as fuel costs. Then there was the issue of my safety, as there are no guarantees on what you might find when you go into someone else's territory. I really had to rely on my intuition to keep me safe. Back then, there was no Skype or Zoom.

On one memorable occasion, I was sitting with a lovely lady at her kitchen table, and the reading appeared to be going very well. I had made a connection with her mother, and the evidence was flowing. It went something like this.

"Your mother is making me feel very cold and lonely, and I feel like I am in London. I also feel like it was towards the end of her life," I said.

"My mother was on her own in her flat in London when she died of hypothermia," the client replied.

Right, I thought, *I'm on the right track.*

The reading continued. Then in my mind, I saw one stick of liquorice. I tried to sweep it aside as I thought, *what can I do with that? I can't say, "I see liquorice." That would be too weird!* The image refused to go.

Then I felt like I could smell liquorice. I again tried to budge the image by visualising sweeping it out of the way. Alas, it was not going anywhere. Then I could taste liquorice. I looked around to see if there was any liquorice lying around that I might have noticed that could be influencing me, and all I saw was a spotless kitchen and no liquorice in sight. Now I was feeling like I was surrounded by liquorice. Obviously, this was not something that was going to go away. Her mother was trying to make a point, and she was not moving on until I mentioned the stick of liquorice she was adamantly displaying.

So, gingerly I said, "This may sound bizarre, but I have to say it anyway. Your mother is showing me a single stick of liquorice. I can smell and taste liquorice and feel like I am surrounded by liquorice. Can you relate to this?"

With that comment, my client burst into tears as she explained in between sobs, "My mother used to work in a liquorice factory, and every night when she came home, she would bring me one single stick of liquorice."

Challenges

This was all the confirmation my client needed to verify that I was genuinely communicating with her mother.

I learned an invaluable lesson that day. To always say it as you see it. No matter how bizarre it may sound. That single piece of liquorice was the best proof I could have given as evidence that I was genuinely connected to her mother.

It is not our place as the 'medium' to judge the evidence we receive. Most of the time, we cannot relate to the 'evidence' as it is not about us; we are there for the sitter. We are there to connect to the other side, deliver the messages they give us and know that the spirit world is never wrong. Where it goes wrong is in our interpretation of what we receive.

When you initially start reading for people, it is ideal to say what you see and go from there. Learning to trust what you receive from spirit is essential.

Responsible Readings and Duty of Care

When doing a reading, it is important to put your client at ease. You don't want them to be frightened, uneasy or intimidated. They have come for a reading because they have concerns, challenges and issues for which they seek guidance. Remember that your words can stay with them forever. Be aware that you have the potential to affect their decisions and life from this point forward.

Too Young to Die

At one of the expos I was working at, I was approached by a gentleman who had been watching me read palms for clients as part of their reading.

"Can you read palms?" he quickly queried.

"Yes, I can," I replied.

"Would you be able to read mine for me, as I am worried about something?" he nervously requested.

I could see that he looked stressed and flustered.

"I am already booked out for the day, and I only have five minutes between each booking. What is it that you are concerned about?" I questioned.

"I just had my palm read by another psychic, and she told me that I am going to die at the age of 47," he stated. "I am really worried. Can you please look at my palm and see if you can see the same thing?"

"Sure, but you're 47 years old now," I replied.

"How do you know that?" he questioned as he looked at me strangely.

"Well, I am psychic," I lightly stated while feeling chuffed that I got his age correct. "Can I look at the palms of both your hands, please?"

He presented his hands to me, and I explained what I saw in each palm.

"You are not going to die at 47 years of age, and no one should tell you such nonsense," I emphatically stated while feeling angry that he had even been told such a thing. It frustrates me when other psychics tell people they are going to die.

To prove my accuracy, I told him the information I couldn't possibly know about that had already occurred. By doing this, I gained his trust and eased his fears.

Challenges

The following year at the expo, that same gentleman sought me out and booked a reading.

"I am still alive!" he blurted out with a big beaming smile. "I thought I should come and tell you that you were correct when you confirmed that I wouldn't die at 47."

"I am very pleased to hear that," I replied with a smile and continued doing his reading.

Nothing can be gained by freaking someone out by telling them they will die at a particular time. What if you got it wrong and put them and their loved ones through heartache while they waited for it to happen? Don't be the scary psychic!

Scary Psychics

Even though some people may express the desire to know when they will die, they may not realise the effect that information can cause and that this knowledge can play on your mind, even if the time mentioned is 20 years away.

I once met a very concerned lady who was told by a psychic when she was in her 20s that her husband would have a heart attack and die when he was 70 years old, and it would occur while he was standing in front of their refrigerator. At that time, she was not concerned as he was nowhere near 70. Now her husband was in his 60s, and that information haunted her. She was visiting me, hoping I would tell her the psychic was wrong. She was losing sleep and very stressed about the thought that her husband potentially had only a few years left to live. I explained that I would not be able to predict the age of his death, but I was sure the psychic had got it wrong; the information did not feel authentic. Dying in front of the fridge was very specific, and in hindsight, I could have jokingly said, "Get rid of the fridge" or "Don't let him go near the fridge." It was easier to joke about later as the lady and her husband are now in their 80s. You can see how stressful knowing that sort of information could be.

Clients who have never had a reading before may be nervous and not know what to expect. I had one client concerned that I would tell him a lot of negative information and had already rescheduled three times before finally meeting me. He is now a regular client.

At some point in the reading, I have found that some clients want you to listen and be a sounding board, someone they can speak to freely without fear of judgement. They want to ensure that what they are doing is correct, or they need reassurance regarding a decision they have made or a situation they are in.

Then some seek your service as an alternative form of therapy.

Remember, you must act responsibly and always be confidential and discreet. Your clients will not want to return if you are not confidential and discuss their reading with others.

You are obligated to be truthful and tactful. You can't just tell people what they want to hear to make them happy or placate them. Even though it might be what they want, they will be unhappy when it doesn't eventuate. Lying to them is of no help to them at all; yes, it might bring a brief period of happiness, and they think you're excellent for making them feel good, but eventually, the truth will come out and then they will be unhappy.

I would prefer that clients feel better after their reading because they have clarity and guidance. In the limited time, which is no more than an hour, that I have with a client, some will expect me to be able to tell them about the last 30 years and the next 20 years of their life and what they had for breakfast to be considered an excellent psychic. There is not enough time to achieve that. I have found that apart from dealing with the client's questions, what usually comes up is what the spirit world needs them to know.

Sometimes, it is better not to tell the client what they want to know if you think it can be counterproductive. One such situation is if you tell someone that they are going to pass their exams, and based on that prediction, which might have been correct in that instance, they change their behaviour by slacking off because they think they will pass their exams anyway. They might stop studying and preparing like they would have done had you not said anything and therefore change the outcome.

Don't Judge Me

As a professional working psychic, I get glimpses into other people's lives and believe me, they are all different. It is an eye-opener to see that so many people have what would be viewed by most as unconventional lives, and they don't wish to be judged because of it. They have come to see a psychic for guidance, not judgement.

Generally, if the psychic mentions information that the client doesn't want you or anyone to know, then there is a high chance that they will not confirm that information, which may leave you thinking that you are off track and wrong. In situations like this, they may choose to ignore what you said or deny it, especially if they feel embarrassed or concerned that their secret will be revealed. They are entitled to their privacy and if they don't want to talk about it then don't pursue it.

The Modern Oracle II

I have uncovered many secrets over the years. Here are just a few examples:

- People who are having affairs and, in some relationships, both partners are cheating and are unaware that the other is. One male client who was having an affair was silly enough to send his wife to me for a reading. His affair came up in her reading, and she had already suspected he was cheating on her. I didn't 'out' him on purpose; I didn't even know the connection as their readings were months apart, and they were strangers to me.

- A very nervous lady with four children, and her husband was unaware that he was not the father of any of them; it came up in the reading as a warning for her as her husband was about to discover the truth.

- A lovely young man in a 'throuple'—a three-way relationship with another guy and girl—was about to go overseas and was concerned that their relationship would fall apart while he was away for several months. They were all living together, sharing the same bed, and his concern was that his partners would grow closer together and not need or want him by the time he returned.

- The parents of a convicted murderer wanted confirmation that it was all a mistake and that someone else had committed the crime.

- A young lady transitioning into a male wanted to know if her deceased grandmother was angry with her.

Challenges

No matter who the client is or the circumstance, when they come for a reading, it is my job to help guide them to the path they desire to be on and to assist them through any challenges they are going through. It is not my place to lecture them on how they choose to live.

Can You Please Tame My Out-of-Control 'Kundalini'?

It is said that the kundalini is a form of divine feminine energy believed to be located at the base of the spine and to be a force or power.

In the early days, I used to teach one-on-one and write lessons to suit each student, something that I had desired and could not find for myself. I surmised that if I wanted that attention, then there would be others that would too. The problem was that I could earn three times the amount for a reading than the student paid for a one-hour lesson.

Then my mentor advised that an hour of my time should be worth the same amount, whether I am doing a reading or teaching, and that I needed to value my time. Around this time, I was starting to get frustrated with some students who would cancel and reschedule last minute at no cost to them. I had a waiting list for people wanting readings and had made my students a priority due to my passion for teaching and developing psychic mediums. I have assisted in the development of many psychic mediums who now work professionally, and I always feel proud when I see them working at expos and festivals.

I took my mentor's advice, stopped offering private tutoring, and decided to teach groups of students in workshops and online development classes, which were even more affordable for students. I also converted the lessons I had been teaching into online courses that students could do in their own time. That way, I could reach more students and have more time to do readings and healing, and it no longer felt like Groundhog Day, with me teaching the same lessons repeatedly. I still have many who will book my time for a one-on-one lesson, coaching, or for me to tune in and work out where they are on their spiritual path and what their next step could be. I love these sessions as it enables me to assist the student in becoming aware of their potential and getting past the point where they are full of doubt.

One late afternoon after a full-on day of readings, a new student arrived for her appointment. As it was her first time attending the academy, I needed to interview her to ascertain where she was on her spiritual journey and how I could assist her in moving forward. I opened the door to a well-dressed middle-aged lady, and after I introduced myself, we went into my office and sat down. I then asked her to fill out a form containing her details, previous studies and recent experience. As I glanced over the form she had filled out, I queried her further and noted the answers on her form. The session was going well, and I already had some ideas of the direction I would take her and the lessons I would add to the personalised program I would be creating for her.

"Sarah, what are you hoping to achieve by one-on-one tutoring with me?" I enquired. "I ask this so that I can be sure of what you would like to achieve from our sessions together."

"I want to grow more spiritually and learn how to take more control," she replied.

"Being able to control your gifts is what many students desire. To assist you further, please explain which areas you want to control?" I probed further.

"I need to learn how to control my kundalini," she answered.

Challenges

Wait a minute ... what did she say ... did I hear her correctly? I thought while feeling intrigued.

"Where do you think your kundalini is, and why does it need controlling?" I questioned.

Sarah started to look uncomfortable and stated, "It is that serpent that runs down my spine and mine is out of control!"

"How is it out of control?" I asked while feeling even more mystified.

She paused and said, "It is causing me to have affairs with other men, and my husband has had enough. I have a psychic friend who suggested I had an out-of-control kundalini. When I explained that to my husband, he got angry and told me to tame my kundalini or he was going to divorce me."

What! Is she serious? I have never heard of an out-of-control kundalini. It seems like she is not taking responsibility for her actions. I was shocked. *How the hell do I answer that one?* I thought.

The more I contemplated what she said, the more amused I became. Then I wondered if this was a set-up and if someone was pranking me. At this time of the evening, I was exhausted and out of ideas. I decided it would be best to kindly send her on her way before I lost it laughing, as something was not quite right with her story.

"Sarah, I am so sorry that you are having this experience. I must confess that I am not an expert in that field, and I don't have the experience to assist you in taming your out-of-control kundalini. I am going to suggest that it would be more beneficial for you to seek out someone experienced in dealing with the kundalini," I informed her while trying to maintain a straight face.

"Seriously, is there no way that you can help me? Do you know of any kundalini experts who could assist me?" she frustratingly asked.

"No, I'm sorry. I don't know anyone with expertise in that particular field."

As I think back, I have encountered many people looking for reasons to avoid taking responsibility for their actions. It is easier to blame the unexplainable to justify unacceptable behaviour. I also encourage my students to be honest and admit when they are unsure of what they are doing or have limited or no knowledge or experience, as I did in the story above. What may not seem real to you may be very real to others. I am always learning, but I have yet to meet anyone who knows how to treat an out-of-control kundalini that causes a person to "have affairs with other men".

Not everyone has the same beliefs, and everyone is entitled to their own opinions without fear of judgement. We are all on different levels of our personal development. Taking responsibility for your actions and not blaming others is essential. If clients are unwilling to take responsibility for their actions, they may look to lay the blame elsewhere, including with you. Choose your clients wisely and accept that you can't be all things to everyone.

The Truth Will Be Revealed

I enjoy working at psychic expos and always meet many interesting people. When I am not doing readings, I usually demonstrate the accuracy and ease of *The Modern Oracle* decks I created. People will approach me to select a card for guidance or for a question to be answered, and I will demonstrate a three-card reading to prove that they can answer their questions with my *Modern Oracle* decks.

Challenges

On one occasion, a couple of middle-aged ladies who appeared to be close friends walked up to me and asked if they could choose a card for guidance. They were in high spirits and seemed to be enjoying their time at the expo.

The first lady, whom I will call Lisa, randomly selected a card from my *Modern Oracle of Essential Oils* deck and was impressed that she could relate to the message. Lisa had drawn the 'Melaleuca' (Tea Tree) card, which starts with the following message: *'Tread carefully and watch what you say …'*

"I have been putting my foot in my mouth a lot lately," Lisa jokingly commented, and her friend Donna laughingly nodded in agreement.

Then it was Donna's turn to select a card, and the card she randomly chose was the 'Spikenard' card, which, in my opinion, has the ugliest image on it. Each card in the deck has an image of the source of the corresponding essential oil. The image on the 'Spikenard' card is of some dark, gnarly thick roots with fine lighter-coloured fibrous strands growing off the thicker roots.

The message on the 'Spikenard' card is: *'You are on the right path, keep going. When one door shuts, another one opens, that can lead to improvement. Finish off what you have started. Not all endings are negative.'*

Donna paused, thought about her message, and then commented with a grin, "What an ugly image; it looks like my husband's testicles."

Then Lisa laughed and replied, obviously without thinking, "OMG! It does too."

Donna's face went pale, and she became visibly upset as she demanded, "How on earth would you know that? When did you see Joe's testicles?"

I could see this going pear-shaped as Lisa became very uncomfortable, and Donna's anger increased. As I scanned Lisa, I could see that she was a lot closer to Donna's husband than Donna had realised. There were secrets there that were about to be uncovered. I had to think quickly as I didn't want anyone to create a scene around me.

"Hey, ladies, if you want to do readings for yourself, you can purchase the deck, and I will be happy to sign it for you. Do you mind if I leave you to it and serve these other people?" I quickly enquired as I turned towards some other people and watched the ladies slowly walk away, both visibly upset.

To her detriment Lisa had not heeded the message to *'Tread carefully and watch what you say'*, and it was now evident that Donna's message was appropriate, too, as I could see *'a door would shut that would lead to improvement'*. With friends like that, who needs enemies?

Unfortunately, now whenever I see the 'Spikenard' card, I think of Donna likening the image to her husband's testicles! Not an association that I want to make.

I Think I Am an Impostor

I meet many gifted psychics who doubt their intuitive abilities. They could be fantastic psychics, yet they still doubt that they are psychic. When this happens, it is commonly known as Impostor Syndrome. Most psychics relate to this syndrome at some time in their lives, and some, unfortunately, align with this and continuously second-guess their psychic abilities.

Impostor Syndrome is loosely defined as doubting your abilities and feeling like a fraud. Apparently, it disproportionately affects high-achieving people, who find it difficult to accept their accomplishments.

People with Impostor Syndrome believe that they are undeserving of their achievements. They feel they aren't as competent or intelligent as others might think and that soon people will discover the 'truth' about them and believe that they are a fraud when they're not.

I can understand how easy it is to feel this way, as there is no 100% guarantee that you will be able to connect psychically and be 100% accurate. Most people I encounter need to feel confident in their abilities before attempting to do a professional psychic reading.

Do other people's expectations make you feel inadequate? I find that people expect me to remember their reading no matter how long ago it was and how many readings I have done for so many in the meantime.

There have been many times over the years when I have thought while doing a reading and surprising the client, *Wow! How did I do that, and can I do it again?*

Sceptics can make you feel like 'the impostor', and it can be very challenging when you encounter sceptics or people who don't have the same beliefs. Anyone who has had negative experiences with psychics and therefore no longer believes in them can also damage your confidence.

Everybody Makes Mistakes

The need to be 100% correct all the time can be debilitating. Being a psychic is the only job where you are not allowed to fail in any way, or you are considered a fraud. Realistically, I doubt that there is anyone who has never made a mistake or been wrong in some way. Most people are sure to make errors when doing or learning something for the first time. I don't know anyone who gets in a manual car for the first time without experience and drives successfully without grinding the gears or stalling the car.

If a doctor makes a mistake, you keep returning until they find the issue or change your medication. I have heard of surgeons who have made drastic mistakes and are still operating. If a hairdresser does a lousy haircut, they are still a hairdresser, and they continue working in their trade. If a mechanic fails to fix your car, you keep taking it back to them, often at your own expense, until it is fixed. I have taken my computer to be repaired by an expert technician and had to pay for many hours, including the hours they spent learning on the job, only to keep returning until the problem was finally resolved. Do you get where I am going with this? Anyone else can make a mistake or get it wrong, but a psychic medium never should.

The first time I attended Arthur Findlay College in England, I had many self-doubts. When the tutor asked me what level I thought I was at, I replied that I didn't even know if I should be here; I had no way of measuring my abilities to know what level I should be at. Luckily the tutor had more confidence in me than I had in myself and, to my amazement, put me at the highest level for that particular course.

When you have Impostor Syndrome, you might find yourself procrastinating or not wanting to commit. In the early days of my career, someone would say, "I have heard about you and would love to book an appointment to have a reading with you."

I would reply, "Sure," and then change the subject and not commit to a time in case I couldn't live up to their expectations. Although once I got started doing a reading and moved into the intuitive energy stream,

Challenges

I found it easy and wanted to keep going to ride the wave of success.

People who don't believe in themselves may never feel that they are experienced enough and will continue to do course after course while never putting what they have learned into action, always chasing perfection. Then some won't attend courses because they don't want to be seen as a beginner or inferior.

It is hard to measure success, and everyone has a different opinion of what success is. Therefore, it cannot be easy to believe that you're competent unless you have evidence, and you can't get proof unless you're actually doing the job and asking people for feedback. Then if you're scared to request feedback because you don't believe you're good enough, you never get out of this cycle.

What Triggers Impostor Syndrome?

It can result from multiple factors, including personality traits, environment and family background.

Self-doubt and negative thinking are characteristics or behaviours of those suffering from Impostor Syndrome. Often, they think their success is down to perfect timing, being in the right place at the right time, luck or the assistance of someone else.

Keeping a psychic journal and listing all your successes is one way of building your confidence and alleviating your fear. The more you practise and do readings, the more confident you will become.

How do you know if you have Impostor Syndrome? I have included a quiz below that you might find helpful. Keep a note of how many times your answer is 'yes'.

Do I Have Impostor Syndrome? Quiz

- Do you set high goals for yourself, then experience significant self-doubt and worry about measuring up when you fail?

- When you fail at a task, do you accuse yourself of not being cut out for the work, or do you feel like you're not up to it, can't do the job and even want to quit?

- Do you feel your work has to be 100% perfect all the time?

- Do you feel you don't deserve praise for your work?

- Do you downplay any compliments you receive?

- Do you like someone working with you or helping you so that you don't have to be the only one responsible?

- If you get something wrong, does your confidence wither, and you feel embarrassed?

- Do you shy away from doing readings and calling yourself a professional?

- Have you done extensive courses and studies successfully yet still believe you're not good enough and don't think of yourself as a professional?

- Have you been doing a job successfully for some time and still believe you are undeserving of your position?

- Do you cringe when someone says you're an expert?

Challenges

- Do you only practise with your family and friends?

- Do you have feelings of inadequacy or incompetence despite being successful and receiving positive feedback?

- Do you always assume you have done poorly?

- Do you feel intimidated when you are with a group of your peers?

- Do you have a persistent fear that you'll be discovered that you're a fraud despite your success?

- When you get something right do you attribute it to luck, think it is a fluke, and feel relief rather than pride or happiness?

- Are you always looking for validation from authority figures like other psychics you deem powerful?

- When you do a reading, do you feel like you haven't done enough, so keep going and going and going?

- Are you hesitant to receive payment for your readings?

- Do you compare yourself to others, especially those you consider more experienced or at a higher level than you?

- If you haven't done something for a while, do you doubt your abilities and avoid doing it?

- Do you sometimes feel you won't live up to other people's expectations?

- Do you find it hard to promote yourself and easier to promote others because you don't believe you're as experienced or an expert in that field?

- Do you feel you're undeserving of any awards you may receive as your achievements are not good enough or not as good as someone else's?

- Do you inevitably feel like you'll be discovered as a fraud or a phoney?

How Did You Go?

If you said 'yes' to less than 10 of the above questions, don't worry. You don't have Impostor Syndrome, just a little doubt.

If you said 'yes' to between 10 and 20 questions, you are well on your way to having Impostor Syndrome. Check out the tips in the next section to help you sort this out.

If you said 'yes' to 20 or more questions, then you have Impostor Syndrome, which is not a medical term, and the good news is that it is not contagious. It would help if you sorted yourself out; luckily, I can help you with that. So that you can be more confident, check out the tips in the next section, read my first book and do some of my online courses that are available at my website www.katy-k.com.

The purpose of this quiz was to assist you in realising that although you may have some or all the above traits, you should know that others are feeling the same at some time in their career, and it is essential to know you are not the only one. These are all issues that I have identified in many of my students when they first come to

Challenges

me, and I, too, have experienced many of them at some stage in my career.

All the above are perfectly normal feelings for psychics to have, and no matter how you score on the quiz, you can take steps to become more confident.

Confidence

Here are some tips to assist you in becoming more confident and believing in yourself.

- Celebrate and keep track of your successes in a psychic journal

- When you don't feel confident, read about the successful times in your journal

- Forgive yourself when you make a mistake and look at it as a learning experience that could help you to grow

- Avoid comparisons; everyone works differently

- Watch negative self-talk

- Say positive affirmations with passion and believe what you are saying relates to you; e.g. "I am an amazing and powerful psychic, and I trust in my abilities"

- Surround yourself with supportive and positive people

- Ask for testimonies, and when you are feeling doubtful, read those positive testimonies

- Know that you can't be everything for everyone

- Know that not everyone is going to like you or your style of reading

- Know that no one is 100% accurate all the time

- Know that you provide guidance; it is up to the client to make their own decisions and be responsible for their actions

Value

Now, this brings me up to the topic of value. People who doubt themselves often don't feel that their services are of value and, therefore, would rather not receive payment. If you don't value your gifts or services, then others won't either. It is common for psychics not to value their services until they deem themselves professionals. Still, the issue is that they may never think they are good enough to receive payment, especially if they believe they are an impostor.

It is optimum for there to be an exchange of energy when you read for others so that your energy is not constantly depleted. If you don't feel comfortable receiving money as payment, consider swapping services or accepting a gift in exchange.

Becoming More Psychic

As you travel on your spiritual journey, it can be challenging to know which path to take or to determine if you are on the right path. Through my experiences, I have endeavoured to enlighten you about what can happen as you continue to grow and develop your intuitive gifts and what you are potentially inviting into your life. The life of a psychic can be crazy and sometimes incredible, but I love it.

By reading this book, you will have discovered that I have had experiences that I would not have thought possible, and over the years, I have often thought, *how did I do that, and how can I do it again?* I know that many of my students sometimes are often surprised by their emerging abilities.

There really has been no structure or set path that I have followed as I sought to become more psychic. I have continued to go from one experience to another, looking for signs and synchronicities to confirm that I am on the right path. Having said that, I do hope that my journey provides some guidance for you to identify where you possibly are on your path and what you can potentially expect as you move forward.

By now, you have discovered my secret, that I am a sceptic at heart. I still question everything, and I am often surprised. Don't be afraid to question what you don't understand, as that is how we learn. Know that everything happens for a reason and at the right time for you. Sometimes you may not be aware of why you have different experiences, and only upon reflection can the reason become more apparent. Timing is important because if the time is not right for you and you are not ready, it may be challenging to assimilate your experiences and learn from them. Everyone is on their own journey and will develop in different ways at their own pace.

I have given you a glimpse into how my sometimes crazy life as a psychic can affect those close to me. Over the years, the muggle I married has become more in tune with his intuition. Tony is now more open to trusting his gut feelings about certain things and has come a long way from when psychics were not a part of his world. I feel blessed that he is so supportive and tolerant of all the 'weirdness' that comes with being in my life, and I try not to freak him out too much. Tony keeps me grounded; in many ways, I would be lost without him. He is my go-to when my energy sometimes interferes with electronics, especially when Mercury starts to play tricks when in retrograde. Tasks like when my phone won't respond for me, he somehow gets it working again.

People go to psychics for healing. There are many forms of healing and having a psychic reading is just one of them. When you are doing a reading for a client, you may be guiding them through life's many hurdles, and this has to be done responsibly; your guidance and their decisions will impact their lives.

Becoming More Psychic

Never underestimate the power of the spirit world. As you can see, I have experienced healing from spirits, witnessed tables walking seemingly unaided and, yes, I have been haunted. As you journey in this realm, it is up to you to set boundaries and learn to communicate with spirit in a language you understand.

Psychics work with energy—spirit energy, and their client's energy. To work to the best of your ability, it is important to be as healthy as you can be, as physical energy can affect your own spiritual or mental energy. Clairsentients get to feel the energy of others, and sometimes that can be very draining mentally and emotionally, as they get to feel what others feel, and this has the potential to impact their health.

Whilst I have given you a glimpse into my crazy psychic life, it is by no means the end of my journey. Undoubtedly, I will continue to learn and have many more experiences that I look forward to sharing with you. There was so much more that did not make it into this book, and the ideas for my next book have been forming. Life goes on, and so does my psychic journey.

I look forward to further enlightening you on what can happen on the path to becoming more psychic.

Testimonials

What People Are Saying About Katy-K

I really enjoyed my reading with Katy. 100% spot on. Thank you very much for the information you gave me, it cleared up lots of things in my mind. Thank you so much.

Eniko

Very insightful and absolutely spot on as to where I am in my life right now. I'm totally blown away.

Andi M

Absolutely unreal. She picked up on absolutely everything—health, ex-partner, new partner—and healed me. I cried; she's incredible. Much love,

Tenayah K.

Wow! What an amazing direct reading. Katy is spot on and covered all my questions and more. PS I'll be back in the future to guide me through this life.

Linda K

Loved my reading, very accurate, precise and full of relevant information. Katy-K is professional and empathetic, and I love her style.

Vicki H.

A fantastic reading experience. Katy-K was so accurate in picking up on key elements and issues in my life.

Georgina

Very accurate, no-nonsense and straight to the point. Gave me clarity and peace. Wonderful.

Sisislia

Testimonials

Wow! Katy was amazing and she picked up everything without me having to say anything. Thank you.

Helen W.

So very excited to finally receive a reading from Katy and she well and truly delivered an accurate reading for me. Will most definitely be getting another one in the near future. Thank you, Katy-K.

Marie S.

I have seen Katy twice now and found her to be very accurate both times, and very helpful for finding clarity.

Nyree

Thank you, Kathryn, for a very insightful reading, you always manage to connect with my loved ones and pass on their messages. At this point in time, I really needed your compassion and empathy, and I was not disappointed. Once again, thank you.

Sandra

Katy-K was amazing, she was so spot on; she answered so many questions I didn't need to ask. I can't wait till next time. Thank you so very much.

Nigel

Having never had a reading before I was nervous ahead of my appointment but felt instantly relaxed when I met Katy. Her reading was such a positive experience and so incredibly accurate and insightful. I will definitely have another reading with Katy in the future.

Sarah

Thank you so much, Kathryn! I really appreciate your sincerity and gentle manner. I feel so much more at peace and able to ride the storm ahead of me. The reading was so accurate it blew me away and I feel supported that someone understands. I would highly recommend a reading with Kathryn. I had a Skype reading which worked really well; clear connections. My world was about to fall apart but now I am clear about the steps I need to take to keep steady and focused. Thank you!

Susan

I was hesitant to pursue a reading via Zoom; however, within minutes Katy had already put my worries aside. Katy delivered very specific, accurate and insightful messages relevant to my past and present situation. Katy was kind in delivery, and I left the session with clarity and confidence. I am thankful and moved by this experience.

Sam

Testimonials

What People Are Saying About The Modern Oracle – How To Tap Into Your Unique Psychic Powers

Katy-K shares her unique and personal experience, from her earliest psychic experiences until now. This is a great book for people wanting to develop their psychic awareness. Quite interactive, with lessons on how to connect with spirit, meditate and understand crystals—cleansing and use—there's space for you to journal your experiences and so much more. You will definitely learn how to access and develop your own psychic powers with Katy-K's guidance and reassurance throughout. I loved the light and wonderful way Katy-K put forth her experiences and how she managed with the 'moguls' in her world. Beautiful words; well done, Katy-K, thanks for sharing and creating this wonderful book for us all.

Rebecca Rane

The Modern Oracle II

Just loved your book, Katy, and have read it twice. It is so enjoyable and easy to read, down to earth and full of information. Just perfect for beginners. I wish I'd had it when I started out, as it would have answered so many questions and squashed many doubts and fears.

Loved your personal stories, as I had often wondered how your psychic journey started, and now I know. I am sure this beautiful book will give so much encouragement to many to not give up and to never stop learning. Thank you seems so inadequate, but it comes from the bottom of my heart. So looking forward to your next book.

Marylene

Katy-K's book was surprising and enchanting. So easy to follow and connect to. The humour in her personal journey and stories is heart-warming. I was surprised at how much I could already relate to in the book. I keep going back to it to learn more and more. Thank you for putting this out into the world, Katy.

Lisa

Wow! Thank you for writing *The Modern Oracle Book* and providing a very relatable book for us to read, reflect and remember very similar experiences of our own. You write in a way that is so easily read and takes you on your journey. This is a must-read for anyone who is interested in the psychic world and would like to enhance and grow their unique intuition skills. I read *The Modern Oracle* faster than any other book in the past. After reading the book in its entirety, I then went back and completed the exercises, which I will return to over time and time again. Cannot wait for your next book!

Sandy G.

Testimonials

Hi Katy, I am so pleased that your book found me. After the first couple of pages, I then knew that someone else has had the same experiences that I have experienced in my life. You could have been writing about my life. You reinforced for me that I was not alone. I didn't even get to start the exercise and messages had started to come through to me bang, bang, bang, just like that. I now have a journal and am trusting the accuracy of my guidance. I am forever grateful to you for bringing this wonderful book into my life.

Joyce M.

Hi Katy, thank you for this beautiful book. As I was reading, I felt like I was sitting on a sofa opposite you, and you were telling me your story. Loved every moment and cannot wait for the next book. Thank you again.

Jo M.

Thank you, Katy-K, for writing this book. I loved reading about your personal journey. It is very practical to read and it's my go-to book. I love both of your oracle decks and need a replacement deck as I use them every day on my clients. Congratulations on such a wonderful book of knowledge. I would love to do your courses this year.

Katie Elizabeth

You are a beautiful shining star, a unique individual. God has truly gifted you with many talents. Thank you so much for sharing your inner journey with honesty and coming from the heart and soul. I can highly recommend Katy's book (a must-read). Katy has written this book with an open heart to let others in on her life's experiences, challenges and adventures. It has captivated my heart. I also love her sense of humour to see the funny side of situations. I was very touched and moved by some of her stories. Katy is also very informative with sharing her knowledge, skills and teachings to also develop your own gifts and skills and to awaken your own psychic powers. Plenty of insight for beginners. I found the book to be highly entertaining and I thoroughly enjoyed every chapter. I couldn't wait to read the next chapter. Just couldn't put it down. It was so easy to read. Katy knows what the reader wants.

Wendy Irvine

I absolutely loved this book!!! It is such a refreshing approach to exploring your psychic abilities and so easy to read, it really is hard to put down. I thoroughly enjoyed the exercises as it gives you a chance to put into practice what you are learning which makes the book that much more enjoyable. Thank you, Katy, for putting so much of yourself into this book.

Kia D.

Testimonials

What People Are Saying About *The Modern Oracle* Deck

I recently received your *Modern Oracle* deck cards, and they are truly a masterpiece. I love their gold edging and clear pictures. They are also combined with messages that give the most clarity to any question asked of the deck. I carry them with me everywhere and refer to them all the time. They are a true extension of yourself, Katy-K, beautiful, clear, honest and a gift to us all. Congratulations on creating your own deck and allowing your spirit to shine.

Kaitlyn M – Rated 5 out of 5

Over the years, I've tried many decks and have been so frustrated with how complex they are to use. *The Modern Oracle*, however, was a revelation in its clear simplicity. Each card provides so much more information beyond its initial presentation, allowing one to hone specific revelation to each individual. Katy's cards have provided a bridge to the spirit realm that becomes stronger with each reading; it still blows me away when I get that connection. Perfect for the beginner. I love them.

Colleen – Rated 5 out of 5

The Modern Oracle deck is fantastic and super easy to use. You don't need previous experience to use them, as they are very accurate and straightforward.

The cards will give you the information that you need.

Such a lovely way to start the day and get loving guidance from your guides and angels.

Kat – Rated 5 out of 5

Well, I do have to say I have over 180 decks; some I use, but I love them for different reasons, but Katy's are just about the best I have used; they are so easy and spot on. I recommend them for experts and first-timers. Even if you don't want to read for others, you can get daily help and guidance for yourself. Thanks, Katy, can't wait for my new decks to arrive.

Jenny – Rated 5 out of 5

I have many decks to choose from when I do readings. Both *The Modern Oracle* and the *Essential Oil* deck are always in my handbag because they are two of my 'go-to' decks.

I have never given a reading from these decks that people don't say, "Wow! That really resonates!" In fact, I had both of these decks

Testimonials

and managed to misplace them, so I bought another set. They are incredible cards, and I find them so easy to interpret. Just use your preferred spread along with your intuition, and you can only give a wonderful reading.

Thank you, Katy-K!

Emma – Rated 5 out of 5

The Modern Oracle II

What People Are Saying About
The Modern Oracle of Essential Oils Deck

I have recently purchased *The Modern Oracle of Essential Oils* deck and absolutely love how easy they are to use and interpret. In one card, there is so much information about the essential oil, the image, the words, the affirmation, the chakra colour and the number meanings. I'm really enjoying using these cards. Thanks for producing such an informative deck, Katy-K.

Debbie F – Rated 5 out of 5

Testimonials

I have both of your beautiful decks—spot on, and usually what I already know but haven't been listening to. I really appreciate the quality and beauty of these decks and the wisdom with which they were created. Thank you!!!!!

Kelly – Rated 5 out of 5

I use these cards to make up roller blends for my friends, and they've all commented on how much they love them! The cards are easy to use and understand—and very accurate.

Beverley – Rated 5 out of 5

I love this deck, and I use them for daily guidance and to select oils to support health and well-being. 100% accuracy, excellent information on the oils, messages are intuitive and affirmations will change your thought patterns; each card is colour coded according to the chakras, and numerology is also in play with the cards. Beautifully presented, and you get to see the source of each oil. Don't hesitate; such a beautiful tool and deck of guidance for everyday use.

Jules – Rated 5 out of 5

From the moment I opened this box, I knew I was holding something special! These cards are unique and something I have never seen before. You can use them for a daily affirmation, chakra colour, essential oil or herb to add to your daily ritual. The messages given on each card are easy to read and understand. This is a great tool to use with clients or to treat yourself to a daily message and affirmation for the day. I also found that the cards blended well when used with the original *Modern Oracle* deck. Thank you, Katy-K, for making such a beautiful deck of oracle cards. My new favourite deck of cards!

Kati – Rated 5 out of 5

My wife has both decks, and they are crazily accurate; I'm always using them for myself, and they are my #1 go-to deck whenever I'm seeking answers. Awesome images too.

Lester – Rated 5 out of 5

Congratulations, Katy-K, on your marvellous achievement to be judged *Runner-Up for Aspiring Debut Author* in the International Tarot Foundation prestigious Carta Awards 2020. This award is well deserved with so many voting for *The Modern Oracle of Essential Oils* deck. Well done, Katy-K, you had my vote!

V. Mason

Offers

- 20% off How to Unlock Your Psychic Abilities in 30 Days or Less available at www.katy-k.thinkific.com with the discount code 'KTKBOOK20'

- Free meditation at www.katy-k.thinkific.com

- Free mini-course at www.katy-k.thinkific.com

Contact Details for Katy-K

Email: ktkacademy@gmail.com

Website: www.katy-k.com

Online courses and meditations are available at:
www.katy-k.thinkific.com

About the Author

Australian-born Katy-K is a spiritual 'junkie' who loves travelling the world, always looking for her next 'energy' hit.

With a family background of psychic mediums, Katy has spent more than 30 years passionately developing her gifts. She has studied with some of the best in the business worldwide and continues to pass on that knowledge to assist others to become professional psychics.

The Modern Oracle II

When Katy is not pursuing her passion, she is driving her loving husband crazy with all the 'side effects' of being psychic. Her other passions are family, dogs, reading, Zumba and saving the koalas.

Award-winning Katy-K is the creator of *The Modern Oracle* and *The Modern Oracle of Essential Oils* decks and the author of the book *The Modern Oracle – How to Tap Into Your Unique Psychic Powers*.

Katy was awarded Runner-Up for the prestigious Carta Awards 2020 for Aspiring Debut Author by the International Tarot Foundation, which has entries from tarot and oracle creators worldwide.

To learn more about Katy-K, visit her website www.katy-k.com

Speakers Bio

Katy-K is an international psychic medium and tutor known as 'The Modern Oracle'.

Having created two very popular oracle decks, *The Modern Oracle* and *The Modern Oracle of Essential Oils,* she then went on to write her books *The Modern Oracle – How to Tap Into Your Unique Psychic Powers* and *The Modern Oracle: Becoming More Psychic – Intimate Secrets to Enhance Your Intuitive Gifts.* Katy also holds the privilege of being awarded the *International Psychics Directory* 2015 Psychic People's Choice Award for best psychic.

With more than 30 years of experience, Katy loves passing on her knowledge and has tutored many students who have become professional psychic readers and tutors. Katy's approach to teaching is that learning should be easy and fun. Her mission is to teach simpler ways to develop your intuitive gifts, and she has modernised the way it is taught with many online courses and meditations.

The Modern Oracle II

An in-demand and engaging speaker, Katy has been a guest presenter at Mind Body Spirit Festivals, psychic expos, podcasts and *Psychic TV*. She also regularly demonstrates her abilities on social media.

Katy currently speaks and runs workshops on the following topics, and each topic can be customised to your specific audience:

- Becoming more psychic
- Getting started on your psychic journey
- Seven steps to becoming more psychic
- Five steps to spiritual connection
- Mastering *The Modern Oracle*
- Setting up to do a psychic reading
- Readings with *The Modern Oracle* decks

Please email for pricing and availability to enquire about engaging Katy-K to speak at your next event.

Email: ktkacademy@gmail.com

Notes

The Modern Oracle II

Notes

www.ingramcontent.com/pod-product-compliance
Lightning Source LLC
Chambersburg PA
CBHW030301100526
44590CB00012B/467